FOLENS

Developing Numeracy 5

Differentiated Activities for mixed ability classes

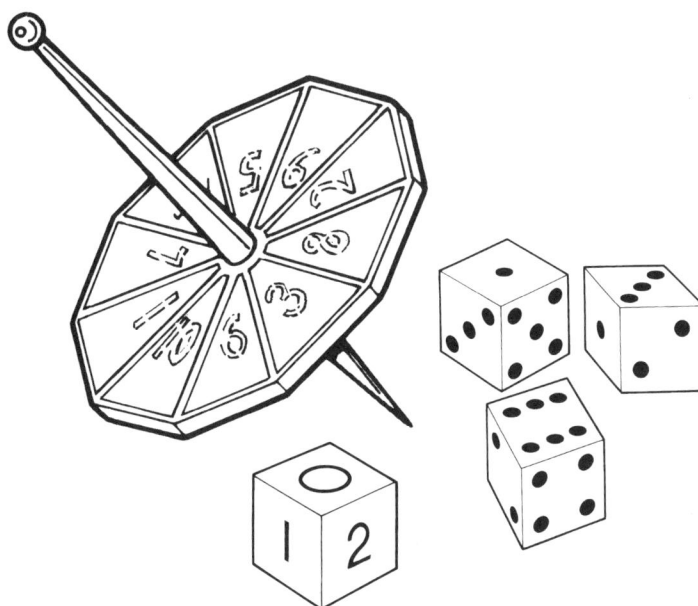

David Kirkby

Acknowledgements

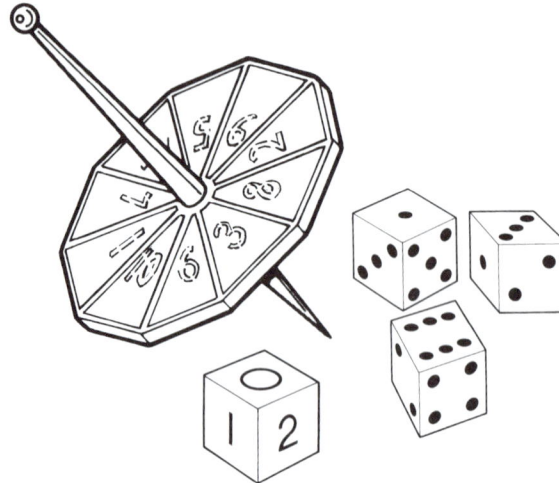

Folens allows photocopying of pages marked 'copiable page' for educational use, providing that this use is within the confines of the purchasing institution. Copiable pages should not be declared in any return in respect of any photocopying licence.

Editor: Donna Cole   Layout artist: Suzanne Ward
Illustrations: Roger Courthold Associates   Cover image: Kelvin Freeman   Cover design: Martin Cross

© 1999 Folens Limited, on behalf of the author.
Reprinted 1999.

British Library Cataloguing in Publication Data. A catalogue record for this book is available from the British Library.

First published 1999 by Folens Limited, Dunstable and Dublin.
Folens Limited, Albert House, Apex Business Centre, Boscombe Road, Dunstable, LU5 4RL, England.

ISBN 1 86202 585-1

Printed in Singapore by Craft Print.

Contents

How to use *Developing Numeracy 5*

Developing Numeracy books provide a wealth of ideas for teaching and assessing numeracy. Each unit provides a ready to use photocopiable assessment sheet for children to complete after the learning and development of each numeracy skill. Answers and success criteria, to assist teachers' assessment of children's individual needs, are provided, and activities to reinforce and extend children's learning of each skill are supplied.

Teacher-ideas page

Clear identification of the skill to be taught.

Suggested activities for learning the skill.

Suggested activities for developing the skill.

Assessment criteria.

Suggested activities to extend the skill.

Suggested activities for reinforcing the skill.

Photocopiable pupil assessment page

Independent assessment activity for children to complete.

Resources

The **resources** required to complete the suggested tasks within the book are centred on those resources already available in schools or items that can be easily made from paper or card. Those most commonly required for this book are:

Number cards 0–10, 0–50 and 0–100.
Number cards 10–100 (in multiples of 10), 100–1000 (in multiples of 100), 1000–10000 (in multiples of 1000).
Five-digit number cards.
Negative number cards -10 to 10, -20 to 10.
Four-digit measurement cards in length, weight and capacity and money.
Money Cards £1–£10 and £10–£200 (in multiples of 10).
Squared and **square root number cards** 1^2 to 10^2 and $\sqrt{1}$ to $\sqrt{100}$.
Percentage cards: 10–100% (in multiples of 10%), 25% and 75%.
Playing cards without face cards.

Number cards in multiples of 2, 3, 4, ... 10 and 100.
Fraction cards in hundredths, tenths, fifths, quarters, and halves and improper and mixed number fractions.
Decimal number cards to two decimal places.
Sign cards greater than/less than (> and <) greater than or equal to/less than or equal to (≥ and ≤).
Marked and unmarked number lines 10, 20, 50 and 100 division number lines.
A hundred square and **multiplication square.**
10 x 10 square grids and **rectangular multiplication grids.**
Number chart.
Base 10 material in hundreds, tens and ones.
Place value boards HTU and **decimal place value boards** in units, tenths and hundredths.
Small apparatus: counters, interlocking cubes, pegs and pegboards, coins and stopwatches.
A variety of **squared paper** and **card.**

Teacher notes

Developing Numeracy 5 is the fifth in a series of resource books designed to offer teachers a range of ideas and activities for the teaching and assessing of numeracy skills across the primary years.

Each resource is organised into 21 units of numeracy work comprising a **teacher-ideas page** and a **photocopiable pupil assessment page**.

Teacher-ideas pages are organised into a progressive sequence of oral, mental and practical activities that illustrate ways in which numeracy skills can be learned, developed, reinforced and extended over several lessons. If used sequentially, the activities maintain a good pace, and offer opportunities for differentiated learning through the repetition and practice of the many tasks offered.

Skill: Each unit begins by identifying the skill to be learned. This enables teachers to plan the focus of their teaching, identify their learning objectives and make the purpose and expectations of the lesson explicit to the class.

Learning the skill offers a whole-class introduction or activity to promote each skill.

The focus is on direct teaching and interactive oral work including counting, chanting and counting round, to practise the instant recall of number facts and develop mental strategies. Attention is given to both oral work and mental calculation strategies before written methods are introduced.

Developing the skill presents the main teaching activity and offers practical tasks and suggestions for working with individuals, pairs or groups of pupils, using a variety of apparatus and strategies to develop each skill.

Assessing the skill enables an instant review of how well pupils have learned each new skill. By each child completing the **photocopiable pupil assessment page**, teachers can make a regular assessment of their progress against each numeracy skill, using the suggested success criteria.

Assessment pages can be used in a variety of ways to suit the individual teacher. They can be presented as:
- a formal assessment of a particular numeracy skill once learning of the skill or unit of work is complete

- an assessment of a particular numeracy skill before learning takes place
- an informal test of mental recall and mental calculation presented orally
- a practice or revision exercise for a particular numeracy skill
- a record of work to form part of a longer-term view of a pupil's progress and achievements.

Children are presented with a minimum amount of text on the assessment pages but young children or struggling readers may need to have the worksheets read or explained to them.

It is recommended that assessment should be followed immediately by discussion with the whole class so that any errors and misconceptions can be corrected and the merits of different methods discussed.

Criteria for assessing the scores and success of the pupils are provided but are intended only as a guide to assist teachers in setting future targets for individuals and groups in each particular skill.

As a guideline, it is our recommendation that children who score more than about two-thirds of the total should progress to a more challenging task given in **Extending the skill**.

For those children who answer less than two-thirds of the questions correctly, and require extra practice to understand the teaching point, it is recommended that they revisit the skill using a different context. Opportunities for doing this are offered in **Reinforcing the skill**.

Reinforcing the skill is for those children who require additional practice in a particular skill to consolidate their understanding of the main teaching point. Suggestions and activities to reinforce the skills are offered, and are presented either in a different context or as a simplified version of activities met in **Developing the skill**.

Extending the skill is for high-attaining children who demonstrate through the assessment activity that they have successfully mastered the skill and are ready for a more challenging task. Ideas for activities to extend their thinking are offered through a higher level of a similar task with opportunities to use and apply the skill further.

Place value

Skill

To read and write in figures and words any whole number.
To recognise place value in five-, six- and seven-digit numbers.
To know what each digit represents.

Learning the skill

Materials: Number cards 0–9.
Activity: Use the cards to display a five-, six- or seven-digit number, for example 25 136. Encourage the children to read out the number and then write it in words. Ask the children to state the value of any given digit within the number, for example 'What does 5 represent in 25 136?'. Repeat for the other digits within the number. Encourage the children to work independently. They should record the number and then write the number in words next to the numerals. Repeat by presenting children with number names and asking them to record the number in numerals.

2 5 1 3 6

Developing the skill

Materials: Number cards 0–9.
Activity: Shuffle the cards and place them face down in a pile. The children should turn over five cards to create a five-, six- or seven-digit number, for example 132 146. They should then read the number and record the value in expanded form by asking themselves how many hundreds of thousands, tens of thousands, thousands, hundreds, tens and ones there are i.e. 132 146 = 100 000 + 30 000 + 2000 + 100 + 40 + 6. Complete the activity by writing each number in words.

Assessing the skill

Complete Unit 1 assessment.
If the child gets:
– sixteen or fewer answers correct, s/he should go to **Reinforcing the skill**
– seventeen or more answers correct, s/he should move on to **Extending the skill**.

The answers to Unit 1 assessment are on page 48.

Reinforcing the skill

Materials: A number chart.
Activity: Using a number chart point at different numbers and ask the children to read and record each number. Point to three or four numbers in succession, for example 10 000 and 400, and 20 and ask the children to say and write the number, i.e. 10 420. Extend by including more numbers and by mixing the order, i.e. 40, 300, 7000, 8, 90 000 = 97 348. Record the answer in figures and words.

Extending the skill

4

Skill: To create numbers to the highest value.
Materials: Two sets of number cards 0–9, a base board in columns of five, six or seven.
Activity: Each child should shuffle their set of cards and place them in a face down pile. One child should select a card from his or her own pile and place the number in one of the columns in the row allocated to that player. Once they have placed their card they cannot move it to another position. The second player then places a card in his or her row of the base board. Continue until all positions are full and compare numbers. The aim is to get the highest possible number.

1	2
10	20
100	200
1000	2000
10 000	20 000
100 000	200 000

Place value

Name _____

Write each number in words:

1. **30 624** _____

2. **26 532** _____

3. **252 047** _____

4. **594 501** _____

5. **1 377 000** _____

Write each number in digits:

6. **Twenty three thousand seven hundred and fifty-eight**

7. **Eighty six thousand nine hundred and thirty-five**

8. **Three hundred and ten thousand four hundred and forty-seven**

9. **One hundred and fourteen thousand four hundred and sixty**

10. **Three million two hundred and thirty-eight thousand**

Write the missing numbers:

11. **80 000 + 7 000 + 200 + 6 =** ☐

12. ☐ **+ 2 000 + 500 + 20 + 9 = 62 529**

13. **500 000 + 10 000 +** ☐ **+ 600 + 90 + 2 = 518 692**

14. **200 000 + 50 000 + 9000 +** ☐ **+ 70 + 1 = 259 471**

15. **7 000 000 + 600 000 + 40 000 + 8000 + 300 +** ☐ **+ 4 = 7 648 344**

Write the value of the digits underlined:

16. **2̲1 634** ☐

17. **16 70̲3** ☐

18. **3̲62 878** ☐

19. **73̲2 546** ☐

20. **4̲95 014** ☐

21. **15̲8 261** ☐

22. **283 2̲1̲7** ☐

23. **5̲26 854** ☐

24. **410 36̲5̲** ☐

Multiplying and dividing by 10 and 100

Skill

To multiply and divide whole numbers by 10 and 100.

						7
					7	0
				7	0	0
			7	0	0	0
		7	0	0	0	0
	7	0	0	0	0	0
7	0	0	0	0	0	0

Learning the skill

Materials: Number cards 1–9, seven column base board.
Activity: Select a starting number 1–9 and record the number in the units column of the base board. Write the number in words alongside. Then multiply the number by 10 and record the result in the tens and units column underneath. Continue until a multiple of a million is reached. Ask the children to describe the pattern and establish that each figure becomes ten times larger and the starting number moves one place to the left. Extend to multiplying in the same way by 100 noting that the figures become 100 times larger and the digit moves two places to the left.

Developing the skill

Materials: Number cards 1–9, seven column base board.
Activity: Use the number cards to generate a multiple of a million. The children should record the figure in the correct column of the base board and write the number in words alongside. They should then begin to divide the number by 10 and continue dividing each answer until a single figure is reached. Describe the pattern and establish that each figure becomes ten times smaller when divided by 10 and moves one place to the right. Extend to dividing in the same way by 100.

Assessing the skill

Complete Unit 2 assessment.
If the child gets:
– twenty or fewer answers correct, s/he should go to **Reinforcing the skill**
– twenty-one or more answers correct, s/he should move on to **Extending the skill**.

The answers to Unit 2 assessment are on page 48.

Reinforcing the skill

Materials: Number cards 1–10, 10–100 (multiples of 10), 100–1000 (multiples of 100), 1000–10 000 (multiples of 1000).
Activity: Shuffle the number cards and place them face down in a pile. The children should reveal a card one at a time, and say the result of multiplying the card number by 10, for example for 300, say 'three thousand' and record 300 x 10 = 3000. Continue through the pack of cards and repeat for multiplying by 100. Extend this activity to dividing by 10 and 100.

Extending the skill

Skill: To divide whole numbers by 10 and 100 to give a decimal answer.
Materials: Number cards 0–9.
Activity: The children should select a number card and multiply it by 10 or 100, i.e. 8 x 10 = 80. Discuss what happens to a number when we multiply it by 10 or 100 (it gets 10 or 100 times larger). Divide the same number by 10 and consider what happens to a number when we divide by 10 or 100 (it gets 10 or 100 times smaller) i.e. $8 \div 10 = \frac{8}{10}$ = eight tenths = 0.8 = nought point eight. Repeat for other cards. Record the answer in figures and words. Extend to dividing by 100, i.e. $8 \div 100 = \frac{8}{100}$ = eight hundredths = 0.08 = nought point nought eight.

100,000

one thousand

700

seven thousand

Multiplying and dividing by 10 and 100

Name _____

Multiply:

1. **10 000 x 100 =** [ ]

2. **300 x 10 =** [ ]

3. **600 000 x 10 =** [ ]

4. **7000 x 10 =** [ ]

5. **4 000 x 100 =** [ ]

6. **6 x 100 =** [ ]

7. **20 x 10 =** [ ]

8. **800 x 100 =** [ ]

9. **90 x 100 =** [ ]

10. **50 000 x 10 =** [ ]

Divide:

11. **60 000 ÷ 100 =** [ ]

12. **50 000 ÷ 100 =** [ ]

13. **700 000 ÷ 10 =** [ ]

14. **70 ÷ 10 =** [ ]

15. **1000 ÷ 100 =** [ ]

16. **200 ÷ 10 =** [ ]

17. **40 000 ÷ 10 =** [ ]

18. **800 000 ÷ 100 =** [ ]

19. **9 000 000 ÷ 100 =** [ ]

20. **300 ÷ 10 =** [ ]

Write the missing numbers:

21. **70 x** [ ] **= 700**

22. **300 x** [ ] **= 3000**

23. **100 x** [ ] **= 10 000**

24. **100 ÷ 10 =** [ ]

25. [ ] **÷ 10 = 6000**

26. [ ] **x 100 = 400 000**

27. [ ] **÷ 10 = 200**

28. **8000 ÷** [ ] **= 80**

29. **90 000 x** [ ] **= 900 000**

30. **20 000 ÷** [ ] **= 2000**

Ordering negative numbers

Skill

To recognise and order negative numbers.

Learning the skill

Materials: Number cards -10 to 10, a large unlabelled 20-division number line, a pointer.

Activity: Mark the number line with -10 and 10 at each end. Discuss with the children how many parts the line has been divided into and locate the position of 0 on the line. Place the pointer at a position on the line and ask the children if it is greater or less than -5, 0 or 5 etc. Repeat for other positions. Ask the children to reveal a number card and place the card next to its corresponding position on the line. Use the number line to practise counting on and back through zero from -10 to 10 and beyond.

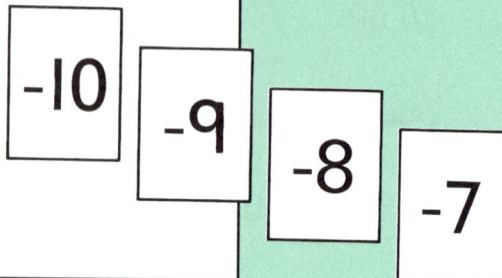

Developing the skill

Materials: Number cards -10 to 10, two blank cards.

Activity: Shuffle the number cards and deal five. Ask the children to put the number cards in order from the smallest to the largest. Record the order. Repeat and increase the number of cards dealt. Working in pairs, the children should take turns to shuffle the cards and deal out five. One child should order the cards from smallest to largest then the other should insert the two blank cards between them. Both children should suggest and record possible numbers to complete the order.

Assessing the skill

Complete Unit 3 assessment.
If the child gets:
- nine or fewer answers correct, s/he should go to **Reinforcing the skill**
- ten or more answers correct, s/he should move on to **Extending the skill.**

The answers to Unit 3 assessment are on page 48.

Reinforcing the skill

Materials: A large unlabelled 20-division number line, counters, number cards -10 to 10.

Activity: Label the number line by placing the cards -10 and 10 at each end and placing 0 in its corresponding position. One child should then place a counter on a division of the number line for the others to record the position of each counter. Repeat several times with the children taking turns to position the counter and record.

Extending the skill

Skill: To calculate a temperature rise or fall across 0°C.
Materials: A large 50-division number line labelled in tens from -10°C to 40°C, a pointer, temperature cards 'Rises' 1 to 20°C and 'Falls' 1 to 20°C.
Activity: Shuffle the temperature cards and place them face down in a pile. Select a starting temperature between 10°C and 20°C (for example 15°C) and mark it with the pointer on the number line. Reveal a temperature card, for example 'falls 20°C' and move the pointer accordingly to reveal the new temperature. Record 15°C – 20°C = -5°C. Repeat for other cards and starting temperatures.

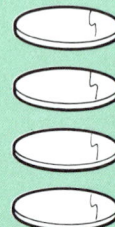

rises 1°C

falls 17°C

Ordering negative numbers

Name _____

Write the position of each pointer:

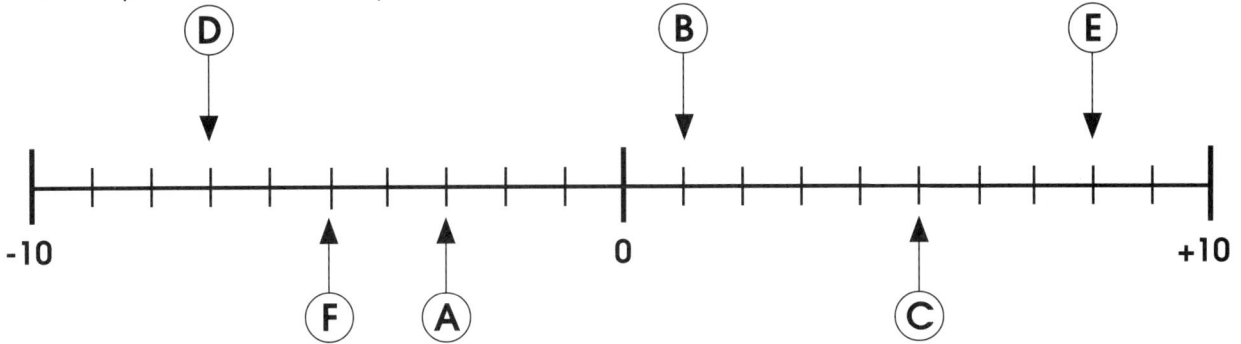

D   B   E

-10   0   +10

F   A   C

1. **A :** ⟶ [ ]   2. **B :** ⟶ [ ]

3. **C :** ⟶ [ ]   4. **D :** ⟶ [ ]

5. **E :** ⟶ [ ]   6. **F :** ⟶ [ ]

Complete the missing numbers:

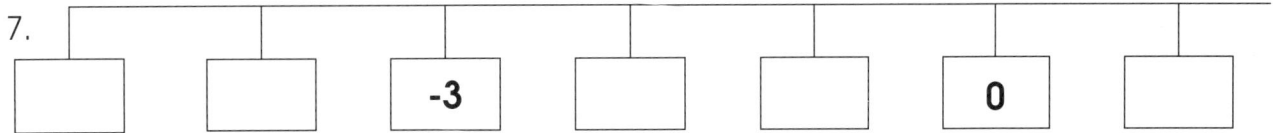

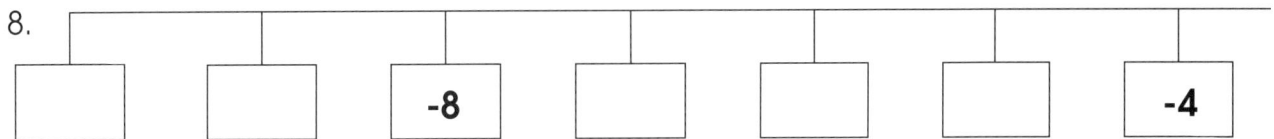

7. [ ] [ ] **-3** [ ] [ ] **0** [ ]

8. [ ] [ ] **-8** [ ] [ ] [ ] **-4**

Record the temperature for each thermometer:

9. A
0^0C
-10^0C
[ ] °C

10. B
0^0C
-10^0C
[ ] °C

11. C
0^0C
-10^0C
[ ] °C

12. D
0^0C
-10^0C
[ ] °C

13.   Which thermometer shows the coolest temperature? [ ]

Greater, less, between

Skill

To recognise 'is greater than or equal to', 'is less than or equal to' in five-digit numbers.
To recognise sets of numbers between another two.

| 16581 | > | 14262 | < | 18516 |

Learning the skill

Materials: Five-digit number cards, > and < cards.
Activity: Display two number cards, for example 18362 and 18484, ask the children to identify which is greater or which is less. Repeat for different numbers contextualised into measurement or money problems. Ask children to select the appropriate sign card > or < and place it between the two numbers, remembering that the number at the largest end of the sign is greater than the number at the narrow end of the sign. Repeat for different five-digit number cards and record. Extend to selecting three numbers and using two signs, 16581 > 14262 < 18516.

Developing the skill

Materials: Five-digit numbers cards, $\geq$ and $\leq$ cards.
Activity: Select two cards, for example 13614 and 15821 and ask the children to identify which is greater and which is less. Ask the children to suggest a number or range of numbers which lies between the two cards. Introduce the signs greater than or equal to and less than or equal to and position them appropriately, with a blank card in between, i.e. 13614 $\leq$ ☐ $\geq$ 15821. Ask the children to suggest possible numbers for the blank card. Record. Repeat with different pairs of numbers.

Assessing the skill

Complete Unit 4 assessment.
If the child gets:
– fifteen or fewer answers correct, s/he should go to **Reinforcing the skill**
– sixteen or more answers correct, s/he should move on to **Extending the skill**.

The answers to Unit 4 assessment are on page 48.

Reinforcing the skill

Materials: Five-digit number cards, blank cards.
Activity: Shuffle the number cards and place them face down in a pile. Reveal three cards, for example 15613, 16217, 17318, then spread them out and place two blank cards between them. Ask the children to record the appropriate signs in the blank spaces and record, i.e. 16217 < 17318 > 15613. Extend by using five number cards and three blank cards.

Extending the skill

Skill: To recognise and compare negative numbers.
Materials: Number cards -20 to 10, > and < cards.
Activity: Begin by holding up two negative numbers, for example -17 and -14. Ask the children which is greater or less/ higher or lower etc. Contextualise some examples to include temperature measured in minus °C. Ask individual children to select the appropriate card > or < to place between the two. Record, i.e. -17 < -14. Extend the activity by encouraging the children to suggest a possible number or numbers which could go between the two cards, i.e. -17 < ☐ < -14.

| -17 |
| < |
| -14 |

Greater, less, between

Name _____

Circle the number which is greater:

1. **17 615**   **17 651**   2. **72 819**   **72 219**   3. **36 122**   **26 319**

Circle the number which is less:

4. **21 305**   **21 053**   5. **30 524**   **28 615**   6. **28 392**   **28 923**

Show the correct sign: > or <

7. **82 163** [ ] **28 950**   8. **16 258** [ ] **18 514**

9. **12 051** [ ] **13 526**   10. **21 319** [ ] **21 139**

11. **16 218** [ ] **17 325** [ ] **12 314**

12. **21 305** [ ] **10 236** [ ] **18 309**

What number could [ ] be?

13. **11 861** ≤ [ ] ≥ **12 215**   14. **79 541** ≥ [ ] ≤ **72 794**

15. **21 386** ≥ [ ] ≥ **18 342**   16. **48 432** ≤ [ ] ≤ **94 776**

17. **30 000** ≤ [ ] ≤ **40 000**   18. **27 983** ≥ [ ] ≥ **18 951**

19. **15 620** ≥ [ ] ≤ **20 532**   20. **57 619** ≤ [ ] ≥ **58 711**

Write a number which goes between:

21.	12 650	[ ]	13 150	[ ]	14 260
22.	26 263	[ ]	26 574	[ ]	26 839
23.	94 716	[ ]	96 940	[ ]	99 999

Estimation and approximation

Skill

To use the vocabulary of estimation and approximation.
To make and justify estimates of large numbers on a number line.

Learning the skill

Materials: A large unlabelled 10-division number line.
Activity: Begin with a large unlabelled 10-division number line. Mark the line with 0 and 10 000 at each end. Discuss with the children how many parts the line has been divided into (ten) and what the value for each division is (1000). Encourage the children to estimate various positions of a point on the line and explain how they made their decisions, for example 7000, 6500, 250 etc.

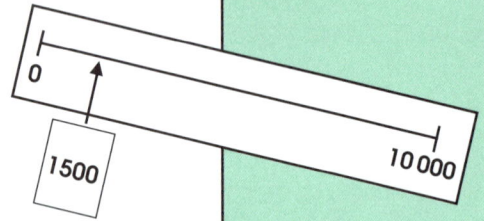

Developing the skill

Materials: A large undivided number line marked 0 to 10 000, a selection of number cards 0–10 000 (multiples of 1000, 500 or 250), a pointer.
Activity: Shuffle the number cards and reveal one card at a time, for example 1500. Ask the children to estimate the position of the number by moving a pointer along the line. Provide recording sheets showing blank undivided number lines for the children to record their estimations. Repeat for different labels, marking the ends of the line, i.e. 0 and 5000 or -50 and 0.

Assessing the skill

Complete Unit 5 assessment.
If the child gets:
– ten or fewer answers correct, s/he should go to **Reinforcing the skill**
– eleven or more answers correct, s/he should move on to **Extending the skill**.

The answers to Unit 5 assessment are on page 48.

Reinforcing the skill

Materials: Number cards 0–10 000 (multiples of 1000), a large unlabelled 10-division number line, counters.
Activity: Label the number line by placing cards 0 and 10 000 at the end divisions. One child should place a counter at a division or between divisions on the line and the other children should write the position of the counter. Repeat several times. Change the labels to 0 and 5000, and discuss the value of the new divisions, i.e. (500). Repeat for labels -50 and 0, making each division -5.

Extending the skill

Skill: To estimate and approximate larger numbers.
Materials: A stopwatch.
Activity: The children should use the stopwatch to find out how many times they can write their name in one minute. They should then estimate how many times they could write it in five, ten or fifteen minutes using multiplication. How fast can they read a page in a book? Use the findings to make estimates of larger numbers, i.e. how long it would take them to read the whole book. Estimate how many words on a page by counting one line and multiplying the number in one line by the number of lines to get an approximate answer.

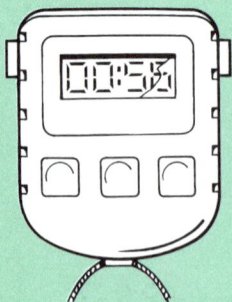

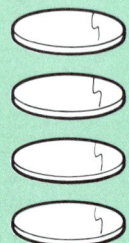

Estimation and approximation

Name _____

Estimate the position of each pointer:

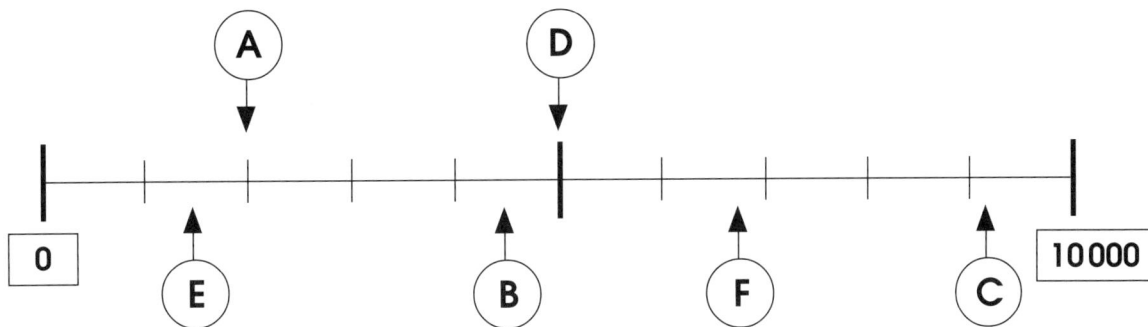

1. **A :** ➤ ☐

2. **B :** ➤ ☐

3. **C :** ➤ ☐

4. **D :** ➤ ☐

5. **E :** ➤ ☐

6. **F :** ➤ ☐

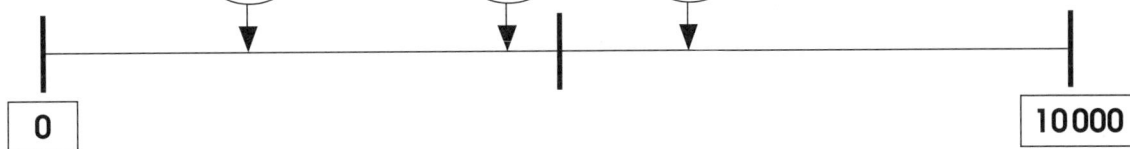

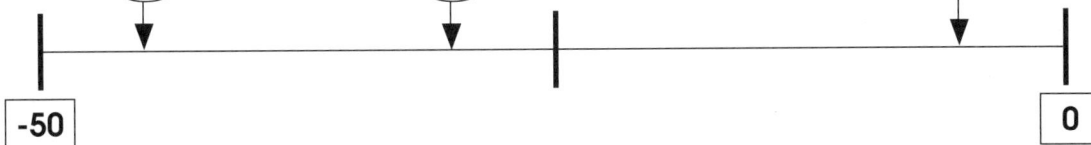

Rounding

Skill

To round four-digit numbers to the nearest 10, 100 or 1000.

Remember:
we round up for
numbers which are
halfway between.

Learning the skill

Materials: A large unlabelled 100-division number line, number labels (multiples of 1000), a pointer.

Activity: Place the pointer at a position on the line, for example 4230, and find the appropriate labels for the end divisions of the line (4000 and 5000). Ask the children: 'Between which two thousands does the number lie?', 'Is it more than halfway between them or less?', 'How far is it from the lowest/highest 100?', 'Which is the nearest 100?'. They should understand that 4230 rounds down to the nearest 100 to become 4200. Repeat for rounding to the nearest thousand. Discuss how we round numbers exactly halfway between.

Developing the skill

Materials: Four-digit measurement cards: length, weight, capacity and money.

Activity: Present the children with sets of four-digit measurement cards in £/p, g/kg, ml/l, cm/m/km. Shuffle the cards and select a card at random for example £4351. Ask them to round the card number to its nearest 10, 100 and 1000 and record:

£4351 → 10 → £4350
£4351 → 100 → £4400
£4351 → 1000 → £4000

Continue through the cards.

Assessing the skill

Complete Unit 6 assessment.
If the child gets:
– twelve or fewer answers correct, s/he should go to **Reinforcing the skill**
– thirteen or more answers correct, s/he should move on to **Extending the skill**.

The answers to Unit 6 assessment are on page 48.

Reinforcing the skill

Materials: Number labels 0–10 000 (multiples of 1000), a large unlabelled 100-division number line, a pointer, blank cards.

Activity: Write some four-digit numbers (multiples of 10) on pieces of card. The children should select a card, for example 6520, and find the appropriate labels for the ends of the number line (6000 and 7000). Use the pointer to locate the number 6520 on the line. Record the nearest multiple of 100 and 1000 to 6520:

6520 → 100 → 6500,
6520 → 1000 → 7000.

Repeat for other cards.

Extending the skill

Skill: To round numbers to the nearest 1000 to give approximate answers for addition and subtraction.

Materials: Four-digit number cards.

Activity: Ask the children to reveal two cards, for example 2863 + 3259, round up each number to their nearest 1000 and then add them together to give an approximate answer: 3000 + 3000 = 6000. This can be useful in helping to check answers. Repeat for subtraction. For closer approximations, round to the nearest 100: 2863 + 3259 = 2900 + 3300 = 5000 + 1200 = 6200. Ask the children to find the sum of each number and compare how close the approximations are, i.e. 2863 + 3259 = 6122.

3259
3000

2863
3000

Rounding

Name _____

Write the position of each pointer, then round it to its nearest 1000 and nearest 100:

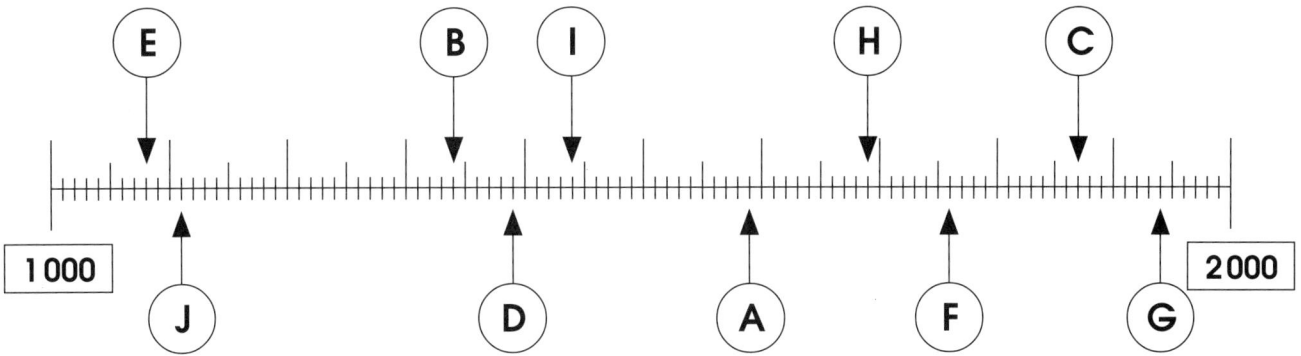

1000

2000

		Nearest	
		1000	**100**
1.	**A :**		
3.	**C :**		
5.	**E :**		
7.	**G:**		
9.	**I :**		

		Nearest	
		1000	**100**
2.	**B :**		
4.	**D :**		
6.	**F :**		
8.	**H :**		
10.	**J :**		

Round each amount to the nearest 1000:

11. **£4700** ⟶ ☐

12. **5800g** ⟶ ☐

13. **6350m** ⟶ ☐

14. **7280ml** ⟶ ☐

Round each amount to the nearest 100:

15. **£3528** ⟶ ☐

16. **1093g** ⟶ ☐

17. **2550m** ⟶ ☐

18. **4602ml** ⟶ ☐

Odds and evens

Skill

To make general statements about odd and even numbers.
To find the outcome of sums and differences for odd and even numbers.

Learning the skill

Materials: Number cards 1–50, in piles of odd and even numbers.
Activity: Shuffle the even number cards and place them in a face down pile. Ask the children to reveal the top three cards to make an addition of three even numbers. Repeat, until all cards are used and a general statement can be established: *the sum of three even numbers is always even*. Repeat for three odd numbers in the same way to establish that, *the sum of three odd numbers is always odd*. Investigate the sum of two odd and one even number or two even and one odd number to establish further statements about the sums of three numbers.

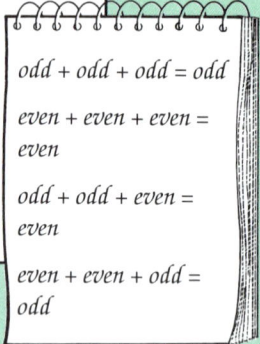

odd + odd + odd = odd

even + even + even = even

odd + odd + even = even

even + even + odd = odd

21   7   83

Developing the skill

Materials: Number cards 1–50, in piles of odd and even numbers.
Activity: The children should reveal one card from each pack and find the difference between an odd and an even number by subtracting the smaller from the larger or counting on from the smaller to the larger. Repeat, to establish a general statement: *the difference between an odd and an even number is always odd*. Investigate the difference between two odd numbers or two even numbers to establish further statements about difference.

Assessing the skill

Complete Unit 7 assessment.
If the child gets:
– eleven or fewer answers correct, s/he should go to **Reinforcing the skill**
– twelve or more answers correct, s/he should move on to **Extending the skill**.

The answers to Unit 7 assessment are on page 48.

Reinforcing the skill

Materials: Number cards 1–50, 'odd' and 'even' voting cards.
Activity: Give each child an 'odd' and 'even' voting card. Reveal three number cards and each child should vote for the sum of the numbers being odd or even – without adding – by placing a voting card face down. Ask the children to reveal their vote and check the answer by adding. Award a counter to those children who voted correctly. Repeat for finding the difference and encourage the children to explain how they can make a rapid decision without addition or subtraction.

Extending the skill

Skill: To find the product of odd and even numbers.
Materials: Two sets of number cards 1–10.
Activity: Split each set of cards into piles of odd and even numbers. The children should reveal one card from each pack and multiply to find the product of an odd and even number, for example 5 x 4 = 20 = even. Repeat for other combinations of odd and even numbers to establish a general statement, i.e. *the product of one odd and one even number is always even*. The children can then investigate the product of two even numbers or two odd numbers to establish further general statements about odd and even numbers.

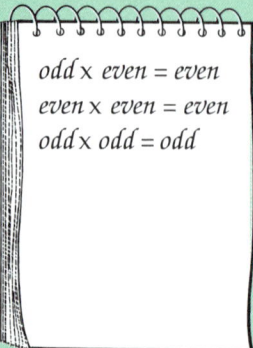

odd x even = even
even x even = even
odd x odd = odd

odd

even

Odds and evens

Name _____

Is the sum of the numbers odd or even?

1. 12 16 24

2. 42 36 7

3. 13 22 19

4. 29 8 31

5. 9 27 39

6. 32 3 18

7. 38 12 11

8. 5 48 16

9. 14 20 6

10. **The sum of three even numbers is**

11. **The sum of three odd numbers is**

Is the difference between the numbers odd or even?

12. 38 16

13. 17 24

14. 35 49

15. 7 29

16. 32 44

17. 26 37

Square numbers

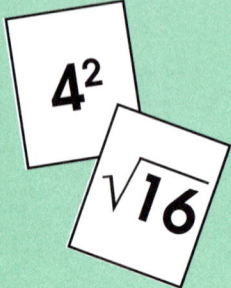

Skill

To recognise squares of numbers to 10 x 10 and beyond.
To know simple square roots of a number.

Learning the skill

Materials: Squared number cards 1^2 to 10^2, squared paper.
Activity: Begin by practising with the children rapid mental recall of square multiplication tables 2 x 2, 4 x 4 etc. Introduce the notation of 6^2 as six squared (6 x 6) and hold up different squared number cards, one at a time, to develop a quick mental oral response. Using squared paper the children should construct squares with an equivalent area to each number card and record the square number and corresponding area of each square.

Developing the skill

Materials: Square root number cards ($\sqrt{1}$, $\sqrt{4}$, $\sqrt{9}$ ... $\sqrt{100}$), squared paper.
Activity: Ask the children 'What number multiplied by itself makes 16?' Introduce this as finding the square root of 16 represented as $\sqrt{16}$ and demonstrate this on a square with an area of 16 (i.e. of 4 squares length and width). Shuffle the square root number cards and reveal the cards, one at a time e.g. $\sqrt{49}$, and say it's square root i.e. 7. Construct a square on squared paper or use a multiplication square to check. Repeat to develop speed.

Assessing the skill

Complete Unit 8 assessment.
If the child gets:
– twenty or fewer answers correct, s/he should go to **Reinforcing the skill**
– twenty-one or more answers correct, s/he should move on to **Extending the skill.**

The answers to Unit 8 assessment are on page 48.

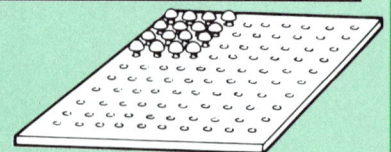

Reinforcing the skill

Materials: Pegboards and pegs, squared number cards (1^2, 2^2 ...), square root number cards ($\sqrt{4}$, $\sqrt{9}$ ...).
Activity: Shuffle the squared number cards and ask the children to reveal a card, for example 4^2 and create the answer on the pegboard, i.e. a square of 16 pegs. Record $4^2 = 16$. Repeat for square roots, for example $\sqrt{25}$, by creating the corresponding square on the pegboard and finding its square root, i.e. 5. Record $\sqrt{25} = 5$.

Extending the skill

Skill: To find the values of squares of numbers beyond 10.
Materials: Squared paper.
Activity: The children should find the squares of numbers beyond 10 by drawing a square of side 11 units, then a square with sides of 12 units and so on to 15 and counting the total number of squares. Record the areas of each square in a table.

length of side (units)	square
11	121
12	144

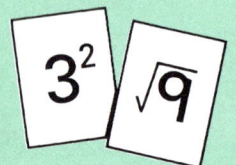

Square numbers

Name _____

1.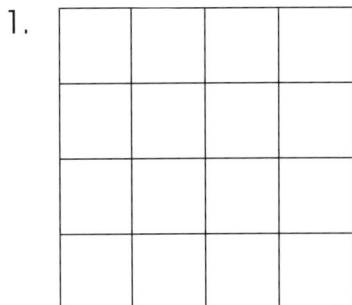

2.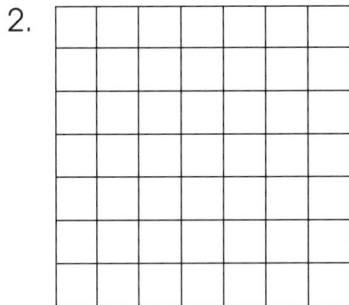

3.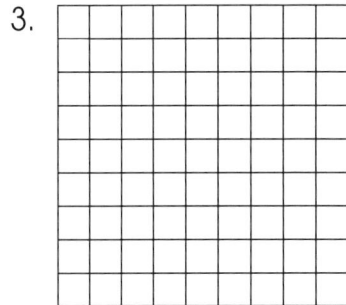

4 x 4 = ☐   7 x 7 = ☐   9 x 9 = ☐

Are these square numbers? Write 'yes' or 'no':

4. **100** ☐   5. **4** ☐   6. **20** ☐

7. **40** ☐   8. **49** ☐   9. **66** ☐

10. **64** ☐   11. **2** ☐   12. **9** ☐

Complete:

13. $\mathbf{2^2}$ ☐   14. $\mathbf{6^2}$ ☐   15. $\mathbf{4^2}$ ☐

16. $\mathbf{8^2}$ ☐   17. $\mathbf{3^2}$ ☐   18. $\mathbf{10^2}$ ☐

19. $\mathbf{5^2}$ ☐   20. $\mathbf{9^2}$ ☐   21. $\mathbf{7^2}$ ☐

Find the square root:

22. $\sqrt{\mathbf{25}}$ ☐   23. $\sqrt{\mathbf{4}}$ ☐   24. $\sqrt{\mathbf{81}}$ ☐

25. $\sqrt{\mathbf{100}}$ ☐   26. $\sqrt{\mathbf{64}}$ ☐   27. $\sqrt{\mathbf{36}}$ ☐

28. $\sqrt{\mathbf{49}}$ ☐   29. $\sqrt{\mathbf{1}}$ ☐   30. $\sqrt{\mathbf{16}}$ ☐

Factors and primes

Skill

To find pairs of factors of any number up to 100.
To recognise two-digit prime numbers.

Learning the skill

Materials: Number cards 1–100.
Activity: The factors of a number can be obtained by dividing a number by 1, then 2, then 3 ... to 10 and finding which numbers divide exactly. For example, 54 can be divided exactly by 1, 2, 3, 6, 9 giving the following pairs of factors: 1 and 54, 2 and 27, 3 and 18, 6 and 9. Therefore, 54 has eight factors: 1, 2, 3, 6, 9, 18, 27, 54. Ask the children to find the pairs of factors for any number up to 100. Generate a number by shuffling the number cards and revealing one card at a time.

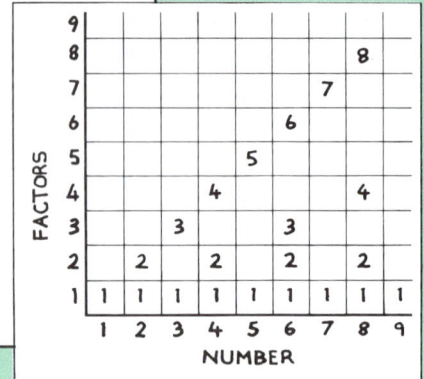

Developing the skill

Materials: Squared paper.
Activity: Ask the children to list the factors for all numbers up to 100 and record them on a graph (begin with numbers 0–25 then 25–50 and so on). Use the graph to ask questions, for example: 'What are the factors of 8?', 'How many pairs of factors has 8?', 'Which numbers have the most factors?', 'Which numbers have an odd number of factors?' (square numbers). The children can also use the graphs to find which numbers have only two factors (prime numbers), and then colour in the prime numbers on the graphs.

Assessing the skill

Complete Unit 9 assessment.
If the child gets:
– fourteen or fewer answers correct, s/he should go to **Reinforcing the skill**
– fifteen or more answers correct, s/he should move on to **Extending the skill**.

The answers to Unit 9 assessment are on page 48.

Reinforcing the skill

Materials: Squared paper.
Activity: The factors of a number can be obtained by drawing all the different possible rectangles made up of that number of squares (whose area matches the number), for example 10 = 1 x 10 = 2 x 5. Therefore the factors of 10 = 1, 2, 5, 10. The children should find the factors of any number between 1 and 100 by drawing all the different rectangles with a matching area. Those numbers which have only one rectangle are prime numbers.

Extending the skill

Skill: To recognise prime numbers up to 100.
Materials: A hundred square.
Activity: Ask the children to look at the hundred square and using a coloured pencil, begin at number 2, and count on two crossing out each number they land on, i.e. 4, 6, 8 ... up to 100. Repeat, starting at 3 and crossing out every third number using a different coloured pencil. Repeat for 4, 5, 6 up to multiples of 10, using a different coloured pencil for each. Which numbers have not been crossed out? (Prime numbers.) Ask the children to look for any patterns in the multiples of different numbers.

Prime numbers have only two factors – 1 and themselves.

Square numbers always have an odd number of factors.

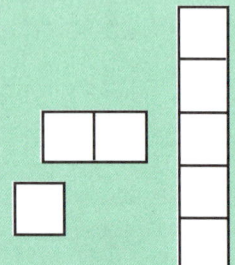

Factors and primes

Name _____

Complete the list of factors of each number:

1. **12** (1) ( ) ( ) ( ) (12)

2. **28** (1) ( ) ( ) ( ) (28)

3. **36** (1) ( ) ( ) ( ) ( ) ( ) (36)

4. **56** (1) ( ) ( ) ( ) ( ) (56)

5. **72** (1) ( ) ( ) ( ) ( ) ( ) ( ) ( ) (72)

Write how many factors these numbers have:

6. **14 has** [   ] factors   7. **21 has** [   ] factors

8. **48 has** [   ] factors   9. **64 has** [   ] factors

10. **97 has** [   ] factors   11. **80 has** [   ] factors

Are these prime numbers? Write 'yes' or 'no':

12. **11** [   ]   13. **31** [   ]   14. **13** [   ]

15. **90** [   ]   16. **15** [   ]   17. **85** [   ]

18. **49** [   ]   19. **7** [   ]   20. **19** [   ]

Colour each prime number:

21.

1	2	3	4	5	6	7	8	9	10
11	12	13	14	15	16	17	18	19	20
21	22	23	24	25	26	27	28	29	30
31	32	33	34	35	36	37	38	39	40
41	42	43	44	45	46	47	48	49	50

Fractions

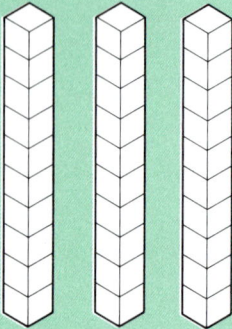

Skill

To find simple fractions of numbers and quantities.
To relate fractions to division.

Learning the skill

Materials: Sets of number cards (multiples of 2, 3, 4 ... 10 and 100 going beyond the tenth multiple), interlocking cubes.
Activity: Begin by giving each child thirty cubes and asking them to find half of 30. Discuss how they found half. Ask them to find one third of 30 and ensure they understand that $\frac{1}{3}$ of 30 = 30 ÷ 3. Consider finding one tenth of the same amount. Ask the children to find different fractions ($\frac{1}{2}, \frac{1}{4}, \frac{1}{8}$ of multiples of 8; $\frac{1}{3}, \frac{1}{6}$ of multiples of 6 or $\frac{1}{2}, \frac{1}{5}, \frac{1}{10}$ of mulitples of 10). Use apparatus if necessary and record each fraction found, for example $\frac{1}{4}$ of 16 = 16 ÷ 4 = 4. Continue through the cards.

Developing the skill

Materials: Sets of number cards (multiples of 2, 3, 4 ... 10 and 100, going beyond the tenth multiple), interlocking cubes.
Activity: Ask the children how they would find three quarters of a number, e.g. 24, using cubes. They should begin by finding one quarter of 24 by dividing 24 by 4, i.e. 24 ÷ 4 or find how many groups of four can be made from twenty-four cubes. Encourage the children to understand that if 6 = $\frac{1}{4}$ of 24, then 3 lots of 6 = $\frac{3}{4}$ of 24 = 6 x 3 = 18. So $\frac{3}{4}$ of 24 = 18. Extend to find other fractions of numbers to give a whole number answer.

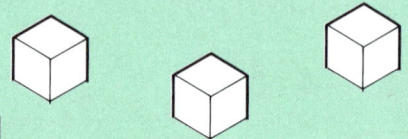

Assessing the skill

Complete Unit 10 assessment.
If the child gets:
– nineteen or fewer answers correct, s/he should go to **Reinforcing the skill**
– twenty or more answers correct, s/he should move on to **Extending the skill**.

The answers to Unit 10 assessment are on page 48.

Reinforcing the skill

Materials: Squared paper, sets of number cards (multiples of 2, 3, 4 ... 10 and 100 beyond the tenth multiple).
Activity: Shuffle the multiples of 8 number cards and reveal a card e.g. 48. The children should find $\frac{1}{8}$ of 48 by drawing a rectangle of forty-eight squares on squared paper and dividing it into eight parts (eighths) to reveal that $\frac{1}{8}$ of 48 = six squares. Extend to find $\frac{3}{8}$ or $\frac{6}{8}$ of 48 by finding $\frac{1}{8}$ and then multiplying the answer by the number of eighths required i.e. the numerator.

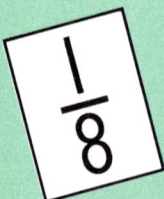

Extending the skill

Skill: To convert improper fractions to mixed numbers.
Materials: Improper fraction cards in thirds, quarter, fifths, sixths, eighths and tenths, mixed number fraction cards.
Activity: Look at an improper fraction, i.e. $\frac{46}{10}$. Ask the children how many tenths make one whole i.e. 10. How many wholes are in 46? The children should recognise that $\frac{46}{10}$ = 46 ÷ 10 = 4 and 6 remainder = $4\frac{6}{10}$. Shuffle the improper fraction cards and place in a face down pile. The children should reveal a card and convert the improper fraction to a mixed number fraction. Record. Extend to converting mixed number fractions, e.g. $4\frac{4}{8}$ to improper fractions by multiplying, e.g. $4\frac{5}{8}$ (4 x 8) + 5 = $\frac{37}{8}$.

$\frac{46}{10}$

$4\frac{6}{10}$

Fractions

Name _____

Find $\frac{1}{2}$ of the cubes:

1.

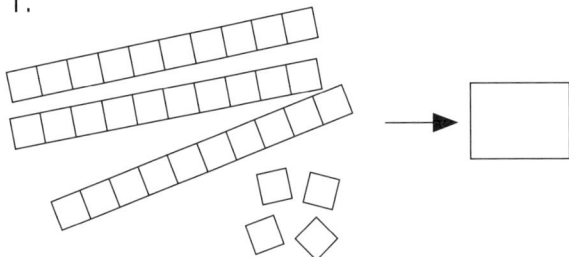 → ☐

2.

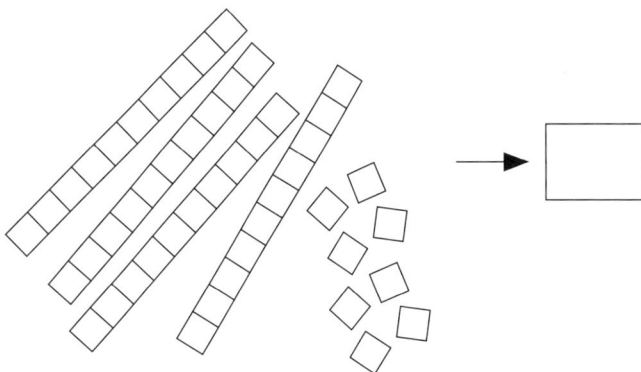 → ☐

Find:

3. $\frac{1}{3}$ of 36 → ☐   4. $\frac{1}{8}$ of 32 → ☐   5. $\frac{1}{10}$ of 90 → ☐

6. $\frac{1}{6}$ of 54 → ☐   7. $\frac{1}{4}$ of 48 → ☐   8. $\frac{1}{2}$ of 52 → ☐

9. $\frac{1}{5}$ of 60 → ☐   10. $\frac{1}{100}$ of 800 → ☐   11. $\frac{1}{3}$ of 27 → ☐

12. $\frac{1}{4}$ of 200 → ☐   13. $\frac{1}{10}$ of 240 → ☐   14. $\frac{1}{100}$ of 1000 → ☐

15. Find $\frac{3}{4}$ of the cubes:

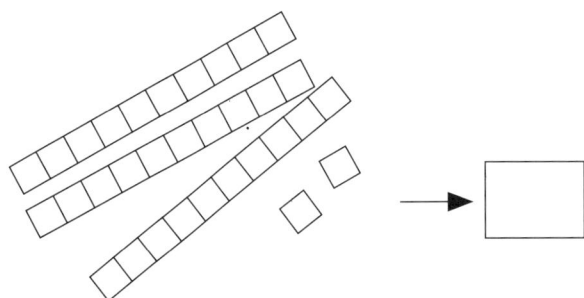 → ☐

16. Find $\frac{2}{3}$ of the buttons:

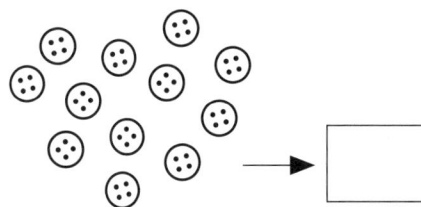 → ☐

Find:

17. $\frac{3}{4}$ of 36 → ☐   18. $\frac{5}{6}$ of 30 → ☐   19. $\frac{2}{5}$ of 45 → ☐

20. $\frac{2}{4}$ of 16 → ☐   21. $\frac{3}{8}$ of 56 → ☐   22. $\frac{7}{10}$ of 100 → ☐

23. $\frac{3}{100}$ of 2000 → ☐   24. $\frac{1}{2}$ of 18 → ☐   25. $\frac{8}{100}$ of 3000 → ☐

26. $\frac{4}{5}$ of 50 → ☐   27. $\frac{3}{10}$ of 80 → ☐   28. $\frac{7}{8}$ of 64 → ☐

Hundredths

Skill

To use fraction and decimal notation for hundredths.

Learning the skill

Materials: Several 10 x 10 grids drawn on squared paper, each with a different number of coloured squares, and some with all 100 squares coloured.

Activity: The children should choose a grid, for example with thirty-seven coloured squares, then answer questions such as: 'How many squares in the grid?', 'How many of the squares are coloured?', 'What fraction of the grid is coloured?', 'How can we write this as a fraction and as a decimal?' ($\frac{37}{100}$ and 0·37). Repeat for different grids and extend to two completely coloured grids and one partly coloured grid to illustrate $2\frac{35}{100}$ or 2·35 for example.

Developing the skill

Materials: A large unlabelled 10-division and 100-division number line, a pointer.

Activity: On a 10-division number line marked 0 and 10 at each end, look at the space between 6 and 7. Then write 6 and 7 at the ends of a new 100-division number line. Discuss the new divisions (i.e. tenths) and ask the children to find 6.4 (or $6\frac{4}{10}$) on the line. Look between 6·4 and 6·5 and point at a position e.g. 6·47. How far is it between 6·4 and 6·5 (i.e. seven spaces or seven hundredths). Record 6·47 and $6\frac{47}{100}$. Repeat for other positions.

Assessing the skill

Complete Unit 11 assessment.
If the child gets:
– fourteen or fewer answers correct, s/he should go to **Reinforcing the skill**
– fifteen or more answers correct, she should move on to **Extending the skill**.

The answers to Unit 11 assessment are on page 48.

Reinforcing the skill

Materials: Base 10 material, decimal number cards to two decimal places, for example 2·37, 5·26, 3·69 etc.

Activity: The children should reveal a decimal number card and collect a corresponding amount of base 10 material, using flats as ones, rods as tenths and cubes as hundredths. They can then use these to convert the decimal to its equivalent mixed fraction, and record, for example $2·37 = 2\frac{37}{100}$. Extend by giving the mixed fraction for example $5\frac{26}{100}$ and converting it to its decimal equivalent.

Extending the skill

Skill: To relate tenths and hundredths decimal notation.
Materials: A 100-division number line, number cards: $\frac{1}{10}$ to $\frac{9}{10}$, $\frac{10}{100}$ to $\frac{90}{100}$, a pointer.
Activity: Look at the number line and label it 6 and 7 at each end. Encourage the children to discuss the value of each division in tenths and hundredths as a decimal fraction. Organise the tenths number cards along the line. Point at a position on the line, e.g. $\frac{3}{10}$, and ask the children to read the answer $6\frac{3}{10}$ then express it as a hundredth and as a decimal: $6\frac{30}{100}$ = 6·30. Repeat for different positions. In pairs one child should set the pointer for the other to record as a fraction or decimal.

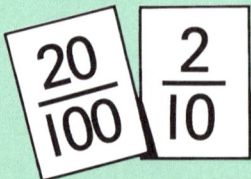

Hundredths

Name _____

Write the number of squares as a fraction and a decimal:

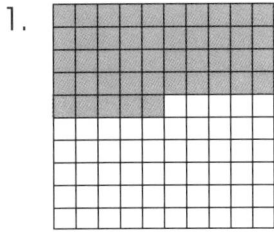

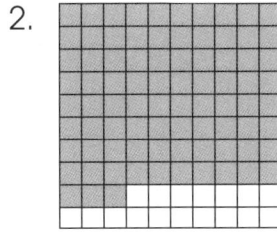

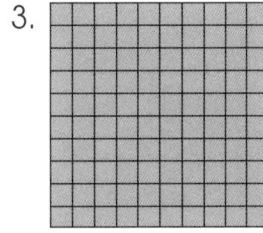

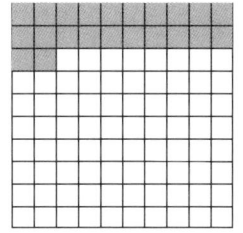

1. 2. 3.

Write these as decimals:

4. $1\frac{13}{100}$ = 　　　　 5. $2\frac{17}{100}$ = 　　　　 6. $5\frac{28}{100}$ = 　　　　

7. $17\frac{56}{100}$ = 　　　　 8. $9\frac{5}{100}$ = 　　　　 9. $8\frac{3}{10}$ = 　　　　

Write these as fractions of 100:

10. **6·32** = 　　　　 11. **5·75** = 　　　　 12. **9·84** = 　　　　

13. **16·41** = 　　　　 14. **7·03** = 　　　　 15. **5·20** = 　　　　

Write each position as a decimal and as a fraction:

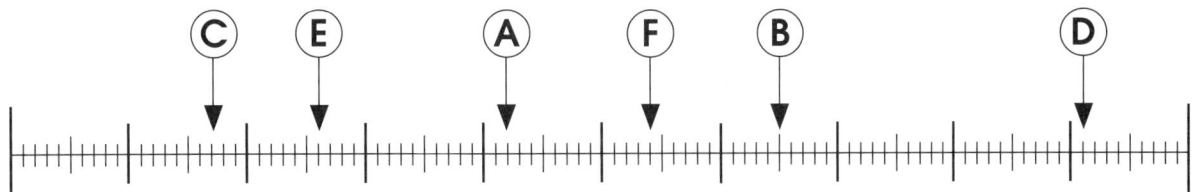

C　E　　A　F　　B　　　　D

1　　　　　　　　　　　　　　　　　　2

16. **A :** 　　　 or 　　　 17. **B :** 　　　 or 　　　

18. **C :** 　　　 or 　　　 19. **D :** 　　　 or 　　　

20. **E :** 　　　 or 　　　 21. **F :** 　　　 or

Decimal place value

Skill

To recognise place value of digits in decimal numbers containing two decimal places.

Learning the skill

Materials: Base 10 material (flats as ones, rods as tenths and cubes as hundredths), decimal number cards (to two decimal places).

Activity: Shuffle the number cards and place them face down in a pile. The children should reveal a card, for example 2·68, read the number and then make the decimal card number with a corresponding amount of base 10 material (i.e. two flats, six rods and eight cubes). Point to any given digit within the number, for the children to state its value, for example 'What does 6 represent in 2·68?' (0·6 or six tenths.)

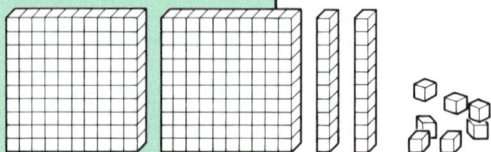

Developing the skill

Materials: Decimal number cards (to two decimal places).

Activity: Shuffle the number cards and place them in a face down pile. Reveal a card, for example 4·36, and ask the children to read the number and record the number in expanded form by asking themselves how many ones, tenths and hundredths there are i.e. 4·36 = 4 + 0·3 + 0·06. Repeat for other cards.

Assessing the skill

Complete Unit 12 assessment.
If the child gets:
- seventeen or fewer answers correct, s/he should go to **Reinforcing the skill**
- eighteen or more answers correct, s/he should move on to **Extending the skill**.

The answers to Unit 12 assessment are on page 48.

Reinforcing the skill

Materials: Squared paper, decimal number cards (to two decimal places).

Activity: Shuffle the number cards and place them in a face down pile. The children should reveal a card one at a time and illustrate the decimal number by drawing 10 x 10 squares to represent ones, strips of 10 to represent tenths and single squares to represent hundredths. Repeat for other decimal numbers.

Extending the skill

Skill: To compare and order decimal numbers containing two decimal places.

Materials: Decimal number cards (to two decimal places).

Activity: Hold up two number cards, for example 3.67 and 2.79. Ask the children questions such as: 'Which is the largest number, smallest number, highest or lowest number?'. Repeat for other pairs of cards. Shuffle all the cards and deal out five to each child. The children should turn over the cards and compare and order the decimal numbers from largest to smallest or smallest to largest. Record. Repeat for other sets of five numbers each with the same number of ones.

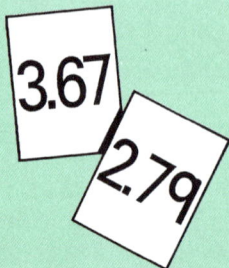

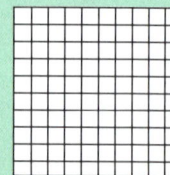

Decimal place value

Name _____

Write the missing numbers:

1. **30** + **5** + **0·7** + **0·04** = [ ]
2. **10** + **9** + **0·3** + **0·06** = [ ]
3. **20** + **0·5** + [ ] = **20·58**
4. **0·3** + **0·02** + [ ] + **30** = **37·32**
5. **0·05** + [ ] + **50** + **0·4** = **56·45**
6. [ ] + **7** + **0·08** = **7·38**
7. **0·05** + [ ] + **10** = **18·05**
8. **0·8** + **7** + [ ] + **20** = **27·86**

Write the value of the digit underlined:

9. **5·32** [ ]
10. **4·76** [ ]
11. **11·97** [ ]
12. **15·58** [ ]
13. **17·09** [ ]
14. **474·41** [ ]
15. **23·27** [ ]
16. **158·75** [ ]
17. **2·04** [ ]
18. **496·32** [ ]
19. **29·08** [ ]
20. **174·91** [ ]
21. **35·16** [ ]
22. **9·73** [ ]
23. **412·59** [ ]
24. **6·22** [ ]
25. **15·58** [ ]
26. **777·77** [ ]

Rounding decimals

Skill

To round a decimal number (to one place) to its nearest whole number.

Learning the skill

Materials: A large 10-division number line, labelled 1 and 2 at each end, a pointer.

Activity: Place the pointer at a position on the 10-division number line, for example 1·4. Ask the children 'What is the position of the pointer?' (1·4), 'Between which two whole numbers does it lie?' (1 and 2), 'Is it more than halfway between them or less?' (less), 'How far is it away from the lowest whole number?' (0·4), 'How far is it away from the highest whole number?' (0·6), 'Which is its nearest whole number? (1). Repeat for different positions of the pointer and different whole number labels on the line.

For decimals which are halfway between two whole numbers we round up to the nearest whole number.

Developing the skill

Materials: Number cards 0–100 (multiples of 10), a large unlabelled 100-division number line, a pointer.

Activity: Start by writing some random decimal numbers (to one place) on pieces of card. The children should select a card at random, e.g. 34·6, find the appropriate labels for the number line (30 and 40), and place them in position at each end. They should then place the pointer to locate the number on the line, and say the two whole numbers that 34·6 lies between (34 and 35), then say the nearest whole number (35). Record 34·6 → 35.

Assessing the skill

Complete Unit 13 assessment.
If the child gets:
– thirteen or fewer answers correct, s/he should go to **Reinforcing the skill**
– fourteen or more answers correct, s/he should move on to **Extending the skill**.

The answers to Unit 13 assessment are on page 48.

Reinforcing the skill

Materials: A large unlabelled 100-division number line, number cards 0–100 (multiples of 10), a pointer.

Activity: Label the number line by placing two number cards at the end divisions of the line, for example 20 and 30. Ask one child to place the pointer at a division on the line, for example 23·6 and the others to write the position of the pointer and round it to its nearest whole number, i.e. 23·6 → 24. Repeat, with different children positioning the pointer on the line and different numbers labelling the end divisions.

Extending the skill

Skill: To round decimal numbers to their nearest tenth.

Materials: Number cards 0–10, an unlabelled 100-division number line, a pointer, blank cards.

Activity: Ask the children to write random decimal numbers (to two places) between 0 and 10 on blank cards. The children should then select a card e.g. 8·26, and find the appropriate labels for the number line (8 and 9) and place them in position. They should then place the pointer to locate the number on the line, and say the two whole numbers the number lies between (8 and 9), the nearest whole number (8) and the nearest tenth (8·3). Record e.g. 8·26 → 8, 8·26 → 8·3. Repeat for each card in turn.

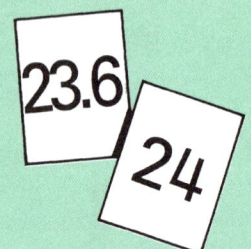

Rounding decimals

Name _____

Write the position of each pointer, then round it to its nearest whole number:

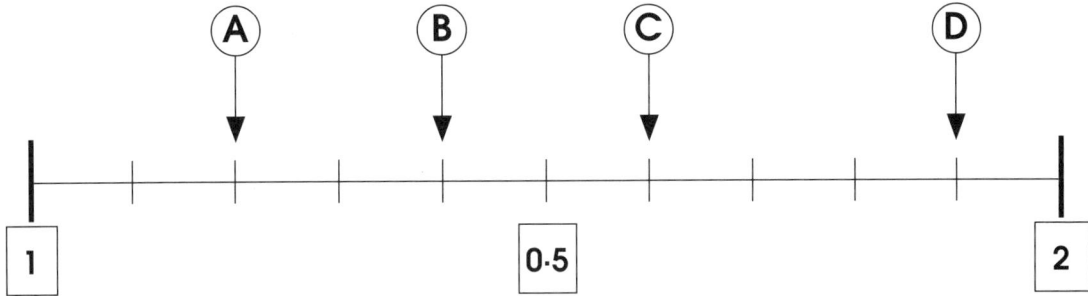

1. **A:** [ ] ⟶ [ ]
2. **B:** [ ] ⟶ [ ]
3. **C:** [ ] ⟶ [ ]
4. **D:** [ ] ⟶ [ ]

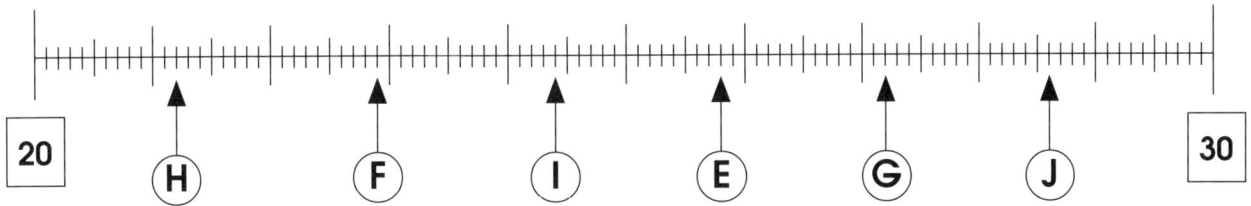

5. **E :** [ ] ⟶ [ ]
6. **F :** [ ] ⟶ [ ]
7. **G:** [ ] ⟶ [ ]
8. **H :** [ ] ⟶ [ ]
9. **I :** [ ] ⟶ [ ]
10. **J :** [ ] ⟶ [ ]

Round each decimal number to its nearest whole number:

11. **2·3** ⟶ [ ]
12. **1·8** ⟶ [ ]
13. **4·7** ⟶ [ ]
14. **25·6** ⟶ [ ]
15. **33·5** ⟶ [ ]
16. **36·9** ⟶ [ ]
17. **12·4** ⟶ [ ]
18. **13·8** ⟶ [ ]
19. **15·2** ⟶ [ ]
20. **10·7** ⟶ [ ]

Equivalent fractions and decimals

Skill

To recognise equivalence between fractions and decimals.

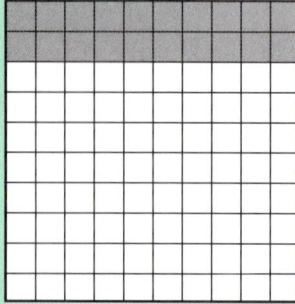

Learning the skill

Materials: A large 100-division number line labelled 0 and 1, number cards $\frac{1}{10}$ to 1 and $\frac{1}{100}$ to 1 expressed as a fraction on one side and a decimal on the reverse.

Activity: Ask the children: 'How many parts is the number line divided into and what the larger divisions represent? (tenths). Place the tenths cards in their positions on the line. Shuffle and reveal a hundredth card, read out the number as a fraction, e.g. $\frac{20}{100}$, and locate its position on the line, noting that it is the same as $\frac{2}{10}$. Record $\frac{20}{100} = \frac{2}{10}$. The children should turn over the tenths card to reveal its decimal equivalent and note that $\frac{2}{10} = 0 \cdot 2$.

Repeat using the decimal side of the cards.

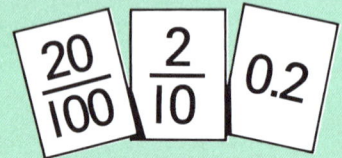

Developing the skill

Materials: Fraction cards: $\frac{10}{100}$ to $\frac{100}{100}$ (multiples of $\frac{10}{100}$), $\frac{25}{100}$, $\frac{75}{100}$, 10 x 10 grids on squared paper.

Activity: The children should shuffle and reveal a fraction card, for example $\frac{20}{100}$. They should then colour in $\frac{20}{100}$ on a 10 x 10 square grid and write the fraction and decimal alongside. Encourage the children to express all equivalent fractions in tenths, fifths, quarters or halves. Repeat for fractions of one hundred that are not in multiples of $\frac{10}{100}$, for example $\frac{17}{100}$, and recording their decimal equivalent.

Assessing the skill

Complete Unit 14 assessment.

If the child gets:

– twelve or fewer answers correct, s/he should go to **Reinforcing the skill**

– thirteen or more answers correct, s/he should move on to **Extending the skill**.

The answers to Unit 14 assessment are on page 48.

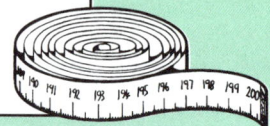

Reinforcing the skill

Materials: 10 x 10 pegboards and pegs, fraction cards $\frac{10}{100}$ to $\frac{90}{100}$ (multiples of $\frac{10}{100}$).

Activity: The children should reveal a fraction card, for example $\frac{30}{100}$ and represent the fraction using rows of ten pegs on the pegboard. They should note that $\frac{30}{100}$ is 30 pegs placed in the possible 100 holes, then express $\frac{30}{100}$ in its equivalent tenths, i.e. $\frac{3}{10}$, noting that there are three rows of 10. Finally, encourage them to record $\frac{30}{100}$ as a decimal 0·30. Repeat for other fractions of 100.

Extending the skill

Skill: To convert one metric unit to another, recognising its equivalent fraction and decimal notation.

Materials: Tape measures marked in centimetres.

Activity: Measure the heights of children in centimetres and convert them into fraction and decimal notation, for example height of child A is 125 cm and 125 cm = 1·25m or $1\frac{25}{100}$m. Extend to the children measuring other lengths which are greater and smaller than 1 metre in length. The children should record their answers as both decimals and fractions, for example 29 cm = 0·29m or $\frac{29}{100}$m.

Equivalent fractions and decimals

Name _____

Write the position of each pointer and find its equivalent fraction:

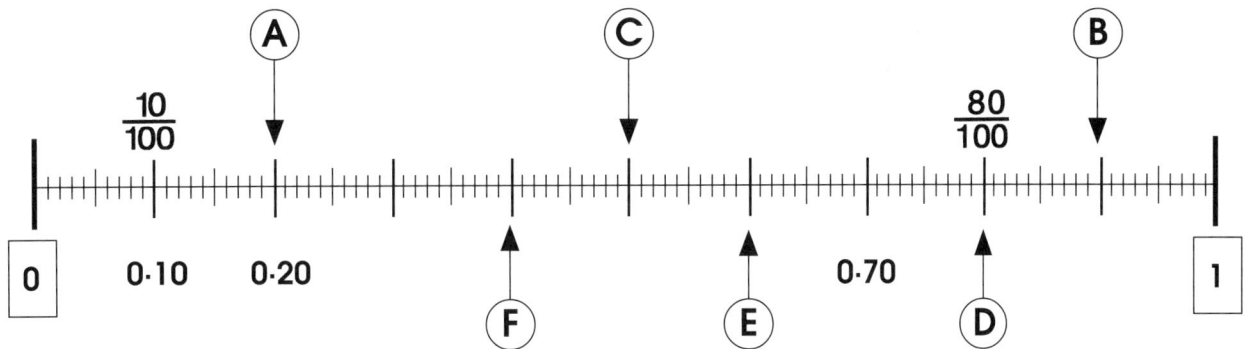

1. **A :** [ ] = [ ]   2. **B :** [ ] = [ ]

3. **C :** [ ] = [ ]   4. **D :** [ ] = [ ]

5. **E :** [ ] = [ ]   6. **F :** [ ] = [ ]

Colour in the fraction shown and write the answer as a decimal:

7. $\frac{75}{100}$

8. $\frac{3}{10}$

9. $\frac{40}{100}$

Find the equivalent fraction expressed in tenths for:

10. $\frac{60}{100}$ = [ ]   11. $\frac{90}{100}$ = [ ]   12. $\frac{70}{100}$ = [ ]

Find the equivalent decimal fraction for:

13. $\frac{20}{100}$ = [ ]   14. $\frac{42}{100}$ = [ ]   15. $\frac{6}{10}$ = [ ]

16. $\frac{1}{10}$ = [ ]   17. $\frac{70}{100}$ = [ ]   18. $\frac{93}{100}$ = [ ]

Percentage as a fraction

Skill

To understand percentage as a fraction of 100.
To recognise equivalence between percentages and fractions.

Learning the skill

Materials: Squared paper.
Activity: Discuss the word percent/percentage and lead the children to understand that it means per hundred (cent = 100). Look together at the % sign and talk about where the children have seen it, for example in shops during sales, and so on. What do they think 50% means? The children should then draw several outlines of 10 x 10 grids on squared paper. Ask them to colour rows of squares to illustrate percentages which are multiples of 10, i.e. 10%, 20%, 70%. They should write the matching percentage alongside and identify what fraction of the grid has been coloured.

$\frac{1}{5}$ $\frac{2}{5}$ $\frac{3}{5}$ $\frac{4}{5}$ $\frac{5}{5}$

Developing the skill

Materials: Squared paper.
Activity: The children should draw several outlines of 10 x 10 grids on squared paper. They should then divide one grid into quarters, and write the percentage of the squares which are in one quarter, two quarters, three quarters and four quarters of the grid. Divide another grid into fifths and write the percentages which match different numbers of fifths, for example $\frac{1}{5}$ = 20%.

Assessing the skill

Complete Unit 15 assessment.
If the child gets:
– ten or fewer answers correct, s/he should go to **Reinforcing the skill**
– eleven or more answers correct, s/he should move on to **Extending the skill**.

The answers to Unit 15 assessment are on page 48.

Reinforcing the skill

Materials: Percentage cards: 10–100% (multiples of 10%), 25%, 75%, a large 10 x 10 square grid, counters.
Activity: Shuffle the percentage cards and place them in a face down pile. Working in pairs, one child should reveal a card to him/herself and illustrate the percentage shown by placing counters on the large 10 x 10 grid for the other child to state the represented percentage. If correct, the child answering should keep the card. Repeat several times, taking turns.

Extending the skill

Skill: To recognise the equivalence between percentages, fractions and decimals.
Materials: Squared paper, fraction cards: $\frac{1}{10}-\frac{9}{10}, \frac{1}{5}-\frac{4}{5}, \frac{1}{4}-\frac{3}{4}$, and $\frac{1}{2}$.
Activity: The children should draw several outlines of 10 x 10 grids on squared paper, then divide some grids into quarters and others into fifths. Shuffle the fraction cards and place them face down. Ask the children to reveal a card, for example $\frac{1}{5}$, and represent the fraction by colouring in the appropriate number of squares on a 10 x 10 square grid. Write the matching percentage and decimal fraction alongside.
Record $\frac{1}{5}$ = 20% = 0·2.

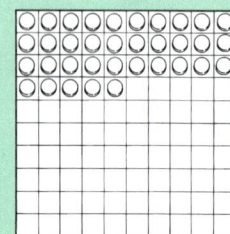

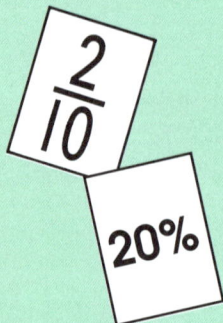

$\frac{2}{10}$

20%

Percentage as a fraction

Name _____

Write the percentage of each shaded part of the grid:

1.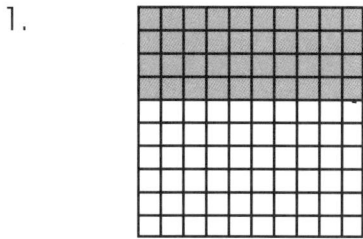

    [ ] %

2.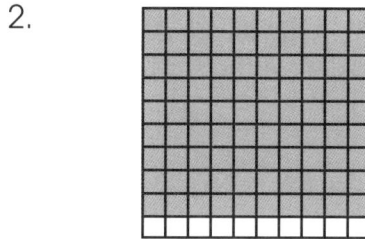

    [ ] %

3.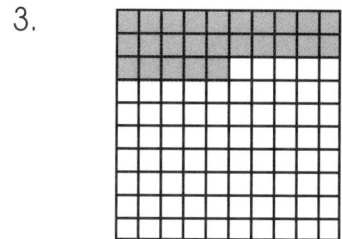

    [ ] %

Shade the fraction of each grid, then write the percentage shaded:

4. $\frac{1}{2}$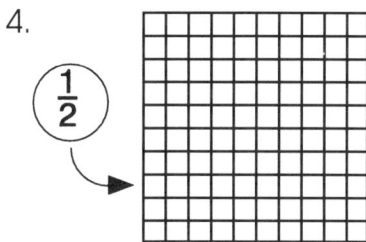

    [ ] %

5. $\frac{3}{4}$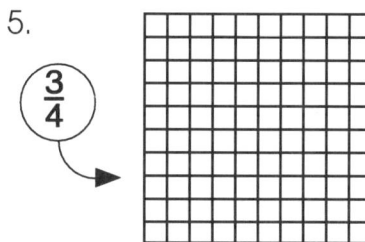

    [ ] %

6. $\frac{7}{10}$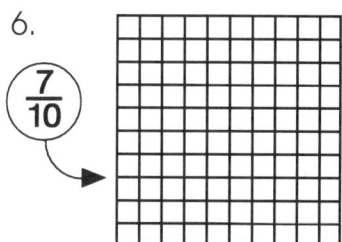

    [ ] %

7. $\frac{3}{5}$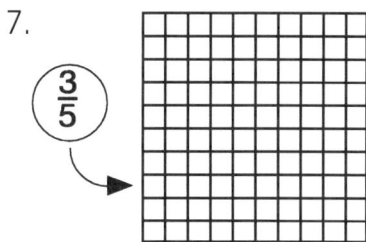

    [ ] %

8. $\frac{1}{10}$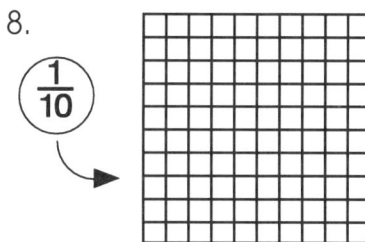

    [ ] %

9. $\frac{1}{5}$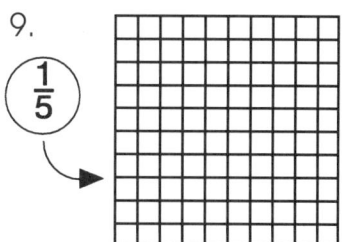

    [ ] %

Write these fractions as percentages:

10. $\frac{3}{10}$ = [ ] %

11. $\frac{1}{4}$ = [ ] %

12. $\frac{4}{5}$ = [ ] %

13. $\frac{1}{100}$ = [ ] %

14. $\frac{6}{10}$ = [ ] %

15. $\frac{2}{4}$ = [ ] %

Percentages

Skill

To find simple percentages of numbers or quantities.

Learning the skill

Materials: A 10 x 10 square grid, money cards in multiples of £10.

Activity: Use a 10 x 10 square grid to illustrate 50% as one half ($\frac{1}{2}$), 25% as one quarter ($\frac{1}{4}$) and 75% as three quarters ($\frac{3}{4}$). Select a card, for example £20, and encourage the children to find 50%, 25% and 75% of it by halving and quartering. To find 50% of £20, the children must understand that it is the same as finding $\frac{1}{2}$ of £20 (£10), 25% of £20 is $\frac{1}{4}$ of £20 (£5) and 75% of £20 is $\frac{3}{4}$ of £20 (which if the children can find $\frac{1}{4}$ they should multiply it by 3 to find $\frac{3}{4}$ = £15). Shuffle the cards and reveal one card at a time to find 50%, 25% and 75% of each amount.

Developing the skill

Materials: 10 x 10 grids, various money cards £1 to £200 (multiples of £10), percentage cards 10% to 100% (multiples of 10%).

Activity: The children should use a 10 x 10 square grid to illustrate 10% as one tenth ($\frac{1}{10}$), 20% as two tenths ($\frac{2}{10}$) and so on. They should then select a money card, e.g. £40, and a percentage card, i.e. 30%, to find 30% of £40. They should begin by finding 10% of £40, i.e. $\frac{1}{10}$ of £40 is £4, so $\frac{3}{10}$ of £40 is £4 x 3 = £12. They can then write several other percentages of £40 by revealing new percentage cards. Record the results.

Assessing the skill

Complete Unit 16 assessment.

If the child gets:
– fifteen or fewer answers correct, s/he should go to **Reinforcing the skill**
– sixteen or more answers correct, s/he should move on to **Extending the skill**.

The answers to Unit 16 assessment are on page 48.

Reinforcing the skill

Materials: Several coins of each type.

Activity: The children should make piles of coins which total £1 using different coins. They should then find 50%, 25%, 10%, and 20% of £1, by recognising the related fraction of each percentage, i.e., 50% = $\frac{1}{2}$, 25% = $\frac{1}{4}$, 10% = $\frac{1}{10}$ so: 50% of £1 = 50p, 25% of £1 = 25p, 10% of £1 = 10p, 20% of £1 = 20p etc. Repeat this for different amounts of coins, for example £2.

Extending the skill

Skill: To find 1%, 2%, 3%, 4% and 5% of amounts.

Materials: A 10 x 10 square grid, money cards £10 to £100 (multiples of £10).

Activity: The children should use a grid to illustrate 1% as $\frac{1}{100}$, 2% as $\frac{2}{100}$, 3% as $\frac{3}{100}$, 4% as $\frac{4}{100}$ and 5% as $\frac{5}{100}$. They should then select a money card, for example £20.00, and start by finding 10% ($\frac{1}{10}$) of £20.00, i.e. £2.00. Then find 1% by making it ten times smaller, i.e. 20p. They should understand that 1% of £20 is making it 100 times smaller or moving the 20.00 two places to the right. So: 2% is 20p x 2 = 40p, 3% is 20p x 3 = 60p, 4% is 20p x 4 = 80p and 5% is 20p x 5 = £1. Repeat for other amounts.

Percentages

Name _____

Write these percentages of £20:

1. **50%** of **£20** = £ ☐

2. **25%** of **£20** = £ ☐

3. **10%** of **£20** = £ ☐

4. **75%** of **£20** = £ ☐

5. **40%** of **£20** = £ ☐

6. **90%** of **£20** = £ ☐

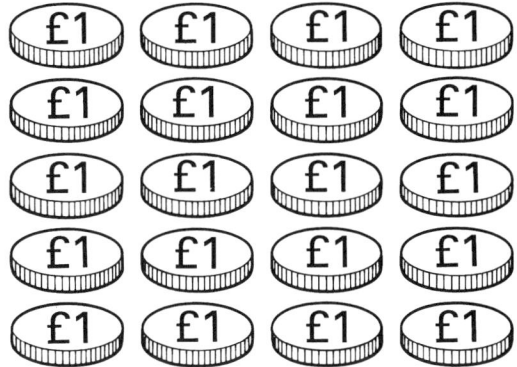

Write these percentages of £50:

7. **10%** of **£50** = £ ☐

8. **50%** of **£50** = £ ☐

9. **20%** of **£50** = £ ☐

10. **80%** of **£50** = £ ☐

11. **2%** of **£50** = £ ☐

12. **25%** of **£50** = £ ☐

Complete:

13. **10%** of **£30** = £ ☐

15. **20%** of **£40** = £ ☐

17. **75%** of **£10** = £ ☐

19. **80%** of **£20** = £ ☐

21. **90%** of **£200** = £ ☐

14. **50%** of **£70** = £ ☐

16. **25%** of **£80** = £ ☐

18. **30%** of **£60** = £ ☐

20. **40%** of **£100** = £ ☐

22. **60%** of **£400** = £ ☐

Adding

Skill

To add two three-digit numbers (HTU + HTU).
To add two four-digit numbers (ThHTU + ThHTU).

Learning the skill

Materials: Base 10 material (hundreds, tens and ones), a HTU place value board.
Activity: Ask the children to create two three-digit numbers, for example 246 and 174, with the base 10 material and place them on the board. Encourage the children to understand that addition is commutative as the numbers can be arranged as 246 + 174 or 174 + 246. To add the numbers they should put the ones together, count how many there are and exchange ten ones for a ten, placing it in the tens column on the board. Repeat for the tens. Add the hundreds together and say the total. Record the addition vertically.

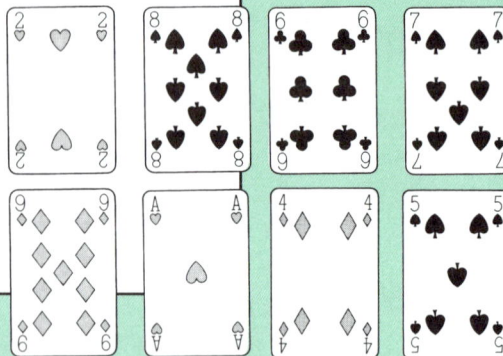

Developing the skill

Materials: Playing cards 0–9.
Activity: The children should turn over four cards to create a four-digit number e.g. 2867. Repeat to create a second number. Place one number beneath the other to create an addition and record vertically. Approximate the answer by rounding each number up or down and adding together. Then add the ones and carry the ten below the line if necessary. Add the tens including any carried and carry the hundred below the line. Add the hundreds and say the total. Check the answer against the approximation.

Assessing the skill

Complete Unit 17 assessment.
If the child gets:
– thirteen or fewer answers correct, s/he should go to **Reinforcing the skill**
– fourteen or more answers correct, s/he should move on to **Extending the skill**.

The answers to Unit 17 assessment are on page 48.

Reinforcing the skill

Materials: Playing cards 0–9.
Activity: The children should reveal six cards to create two three-digit numbers, for example 163 and 821. They should then place one number beneath the other to create an addition, and approximate the answer by rounding each number up or down and adding, for example 200 + 800 = 1000. Begin by adding the most significant digits first, i.e. hundreds, tens and then ones, recording each separately and then adding them together mentally from the top.

Extending the skill

Skill: To add two decimal fractions with and without carrying.
Materials: A decimal place-value board, number cards 0–9, base 10 material (flats, rods, cubes).
Activity: Place two numbers in base 10 material on the place value board using flats as units or ones, rods as tenths and cubes as hundredths. Begin adding the hundredths by putting the cubes together and exchange ten cubes for a tenth or rod. Repeat for the tenths then add the units. Record the addition vertically, carrying the 1's below the line and understanding that decimal points should line up under each other. Repeat using number cards on the board and recording in the same way.

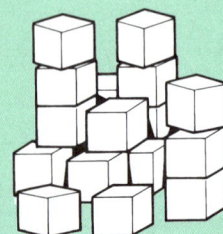

U	•	t	h

Adding

Name _____

Approximate and add:

1.
| Approximate 500 |
```
  2 1 6
+ 3 4 4
_____
```

2.
| |
```
  3 2 5
+ 4 6 8
_____
```

3.
| |
```
  7 4 6
+ 2 3 6
_____
```

4.
| |
```
  8 3 4
+ 1 2 9
_____
```

5.
| |
```
  3 4 7
+ 2 7 8
_____
```

6.
| |
```
  2 7 9
+ 3 6 4
_____
```

7.
| |
```
  8 9 3
+ 1 2 7
_____
```

8.
| |
```
  2 7 5
+ 3 9 6
_____
```

9.
| |
```
  3 2 7 6
+ 4 1 3 4
_____
```

10.
| |
```
  2 1 8 4
+ 1 2 7 7
_____
```

11.
| |
```
  1 3 0 7
+ 2 8 4 8
_____
```

12.
| |
```
  2 5 3 3
+ 4 2 9 1
_____
```

Write the missing numbers:

13.
```
  3 2 3
+ 1 □ 4
_____
  4 5 7
```

14.
```
  □ 2 7
+ 4 7 2
_____
  8 9 9
```

15.
```
  2 4 6
+ 7 3 □
_____
  9 8 0
```

16.
```
  7 1 3
+ 1 □ 8
_____
  8 9 1
```

17.
```
  2 4 3 8
+ 4 3 6 □
_____
□ 8 0 2
```

18.
```
  1 2 8 7
+ 3 3 4 8
_____
□ 6 □ 5
```

19.
```
  □ □ 3 7
+ 2 2 3 4
_____
  8 7 7 □
```

20.
```
  2 3 □ 9
+ 5 1 4 3
_____
  7 □ 0 2
```

Subtracting

Skill

To subtract one three-digit number from another (with adjustment).
To subtract one four-digit number from another (with adjustment).

Subtraction is not commutative: 576 – 143 is not the same as 143 – 576.

Learning the skill

Materials: Base 10 material (hundreds, tens and ones), a HTU place-value board.
Activity: Ask the children to create a three-digit number with the base 10 material and place it on the board. Subtract the required number of ones by taking them away from the units column, and if there are not enough, exchange one of the tens for ten ones then proceed to subtract. Count how many ones there are left and record vertically. Repeat for subtracting the tens, exchanging a hundred for ten tens if necessary. Finally, subtract the hundreds and record. Say the number which is left.

Developing the skill

Materials: Playing cards 0–9.
Activity: The children should turn over eight cards to create two four-digit numbers, arrange the smaller of the two numbers beneath the larger to create a subtraction. Approximate the answer by rounding each number up or down and subtracting the smaller from the larger. Perform the subtraction by recording it vertically and subtracting the ones first, decompose the tens and hundreds if necessary. Say the answer and compare with the approximation.

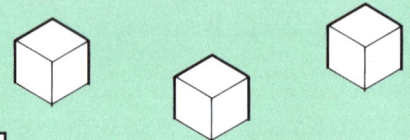

Assessing the skill

Complete Unit 18 assessment.
If the child gets:
– thirteen or fewer answers correct, s/he should go to **Reinforcing the skill**
– fourteen or more answers correct, s/he should move on to **Extending the skill.**

The answers to Unit 18 assessment are on page 48.

Reinforcing the skill

Materials: Playing cards 0–9.
Activity: The children should take three cards from the pile to create a three-digit number. Repeat to generate a second number and arrange to create a subtraction of the smaller number from the larger, for example 724–268. Approximate the answer then record the subtraction by splitting each number separately into hundreds, tens and ones. Check by comparing the answer with the approximation.

$$
\begin{array}{r}
724 - 268 \\
\hline
700 + 20 + 4 \\
- 200 + 60 + 8 \\
\hline
700 + 10 + 14 \\
- 200 + 60 + 8 \\
\hline
600 + 110 + 14 \\
- 200 + 60 + 8 \\
\hline
400 + 50 + 6 \\
= 456
\end{array}
$$

Extending the skill

Skill: To subtract one decimal fraction from another.
Materials: A decimal place value board, base 10 material (flats, rods and cubes).
Activity: Create a decimal number (to two decimal places) in base 10 material on the place value board. The children should then subtract the required number of hundredths by taking them from the hundredths column and, borrowing ten tenths from the tenths column if there are not enough. Repeat for tenths. Finally subtract the units and record the answer vertically understanding that the decimal points should line up under each other. Repeat for other subtractions.

U	t	h

Subtracting

Name _____

Approximate and subtract:

1.
| Approximate 100 |

```
  3 2 6
- 2 1 3
_____

_____
```

2.
| |

```
  5 9 4
- 2 8 2
_____

_____
```

3.
| |

```
  8 3 8
- 1 1 5
_____

_____
```

4.
| |

```
  2 7 9
- 1 2 3
_____

_____
```

5.
| |

```
  4 5 3
- 3 1 7
_____

_____
```

6.
| |

```
  6 7 2
- 3 5 8
_____

_____
```

7.
| |

```
  2 8 0
- 1 3 5
_____

_____
```

8.
| |

```
  8 8 7
- 2 4 8
_____

_____
```

9.
| |

```
  5 2 1
- 2 3 6
_____

_____
```

10.
| |

```
  2 6 3
- 1 8 9
_____

_____
```

11.
| |

```
  8 2 2
- 4 7 7
_____

_____
```

12.
| |

```
  9 0 7
- 3 2 8
_____

_____
```

13.
| |

```
  4 3 7 3
- 2 1 3 4
_____

_____
```

14.
| |

```
  5 6 8 4
- 1 2 8 5
_____

_____
```

15.
| |

```
  4 8 9 1
- 2 3 8 3
_____

_____
```

16.
| |

```
  5 4 7 5
- 4 1 3 7
_____

_____
```

17.
| |

```
  8 3 2 0
- 4 4 3 5
_____

_____
```

18.
| |

```
  8 5 3 5
- 2 8 4 6
_____

_____
```

19.
| |

```
  9 8 3 5
- 7 9 5 9
_____

_____
```

20.
| |

```
  5 2 1 6
- 3 7 2 8
_____

_____
```

Multiplying to 10 x 10

Skill

To recall multiplication facts up to 10 x 10.

Learning the skill

Materials: Rectangular grids for each of the multiplication facts up to 10 x 10.

Activity: Choose a rectangular grid, for example 6 x 8. Ask the children questions such as: 'How many rows?', 'How many squares in each row?', 'How many squares altogether?'. The children should then record this as 6 x 8 = 48. Illustrate counting in eights by pointing at each row as you count. Rotate the grid and repeat to illustrate that 6 x 8 = 8 x 6 = 48. This enables children to switch the multiplication to make it easier. Repeat for other grids.

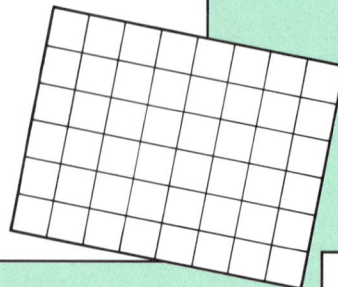

6 x 8

Developing the skill

Materials: Two sets of number cards 1–10, a multiplication square.

Activity: Using the multiplication square, the children should practise saying the multiples of 4, for example using the fourth row as a check. Point to a number along the first row, e.g. 6, and the children should say 'six fours are twenty-four', then check by counting along the fourth row. Shuffle the cards into two piles. The children should reveal the top card from each pile to create a multiplication. Record it and write the answer then check as described.

Assessing the skill

Complete Unit 19 assessment.
If the child gets:
– thirteen or fewer answers correct, s/he should go to **Reinforcing the skill**
– fourteen or more answers correct, s/he should move on to **Extending the skill**.

The answers to Unit 19 assessment are on page 48.

Reinforcing the skill

Materials: Pegboards and pegs, number cards 1–10.

Activity: Shuffle the number cards and place them face down in a pile. The children should reveal two cards to create a multiplication, for example 5 x 8 then match the multiplication by creating a rectangular arrangement of pegs on the pegboard, for example for 5 x 8 create five rows of eight pegs. They should then find the answer to their multiplication by counting the total number of pegs used. Repeat for other multiplications. Record.

Extending the skill

Skill: To multiply three one-digit numbers.
Materials: Three dice.
Activity: Teach the children the method of multiplying three numbers by first multiplying two together and then multiplying the answer by the third. The children should throw the three dice, for example 6, 5, 2 and choose any two to multiply together, i.e. 6 x 5 = 30. Then multiply the answer by the third dice, i.e. 30 x 2 = 60. Keeping the same dice throw, encourage the children to experiment by starting with a different pair of numbers, for example 6 x 2 or 5 x 2, to demonstrate that the final answer is the same. Record each combination. Repeat.

$2 \times 3 \times 4 = 6 \times 4 = 24$

$2 \times 4 \times 3 = 8 \times 3 = 24$

$3 \times 4 \times 2 = 12 \times 2 = 24$

Multiplying to 10 x 10

Name _____

Complete these multiplication tables:

1.

[ ] x [ ] = [ ]

2.

[ ] x [ ] = [ ]

3.

x	2	8	4	6
7				
3				
5				
1				

4.

x	6	8	7	9
8				
6				
9				
7				

Complete:

5. **6** x **4** = [ ]

6. **8** x **5** = [ ]

7. **7** x **4** = [ ]

8. **9** x **4** = [ ]

9. **3** x **7** = [ ]

10. **10** x **7** = [ ]

11. **5** x **6** = [ ]

12. **7** x **6** = [ ]

Write the missing numbers:

13. **5** x [ ] = **45**

14. **7** x [ ] = **42**

15. [ ] x **9** = **36**

16. [ ] x **8** = **24**

17. **5** x [ ] = **35**

18. [ ] x **7** = **49**

19. [ ] x **6** = **54**

20. **10** x [ ] = **30**

Multiplying

Skill

To multiply a two-digit and a three-digit number by a one-digit number (TU X U, HTU X U).

Learning the skill

Activity: As a whole class, consider multiplying a two-digit number by a one-digit number, for example 23 x 6. Explain to the children how they can split 23 into its separate tens and ones, i.e. 20 + 3, and then illustrate the multiplication as a rectangle. The children should then multiply each part of 23 separately by 6, recording the results in each part of the rectangle. They can add the results together vertically to find the answer. Repeat for different multiplications. Extend to multiplying a three-digit number by a one-digit number (HTU X U), by splitting the number into three parts.

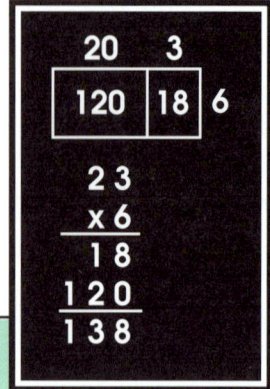

Developing the skill

Materials: Number cards 0–9.
Activity: Ask the children to reveal three cards to create a three-digit number, for example 532. They should then reveal another card to act as a multiplier, for example 6. The children should make an estimate of the answer by saying that 532 x 6 is about 500 x 6 which is 3000. Record the estimate. They should then split the three-digit number into three parts and multiply each part by 6. Draw a rectangle to record the multiplication. Compare the answer with the estimate. Repeat, for other three-digit numbers.

Assessing the skill

Complete Unit 20 assessment.
If the child gets:
– five or fewer answers correct, s/he should go to **Reinforcing the skill**
– six or more answers correct, s/he should move on to **Extending the skill**.

The answers to Unit 20 assessment are on page 48.

Reinforcing the skill

Materials: Base 10 material (hundreds, tens and ones).
Activity: The children should use the base 10 material to illustrate a multiplication, for example for 4 x 36. They should start by building four sets of thirty-six with the material, then put all the material together, changing ten ones for a tens-rod, or ten tens rods for a hundred if necessary. They should then count the material to find the answer to the multiplication and record. Repeat for three-digit numbers.

Extending the skill

Skill: To multiply a two-digit number by a two-digit number TU x TU.
Activity: Encourage the children to consider a TU x TU multiplication, for example 21 x 38. They should start by estimating the answer by saying that it is about 20 x 40 (twenty lots of four tens is eighty tens) = 800. They should then split both numbers into their separate tens and ones, i.e. 20 + 1 and 30 + 8. Illustrate the multiplication as a rectangle and multiply each part separately, recording the results in each part of the rectangle. Record and add the results together vertically. Compare the correct answer with the estimate.

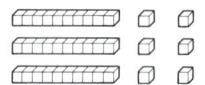

Multiplying

Name _____

Multiply:

1.

30	X
	3

30 x 3 = [ ]

2.

20	3	X
		6

[ ] x [ ] = [ ]

3.

40	2	X
		7

[ ] x [ ] = [ ]

4.

30	6	X
		5

[ ] x [ ] = [ ]

5.

300	20	1	X
			8

321 x 8 = [ ]

6.

200	80	6	X
			4

[ ] x [ ] = [ ]

7.

400	20	3	X
			5

[ ] x [ ] = [ ]

8.

100	50	6	X
			7

[ ] x [ ] = [ ]

Dividing

Skill

To divide a two-digit number by a one-digit number (TU ÷ U).
To divide a three-digit number by a one-digit number
(HTU ÷ U).

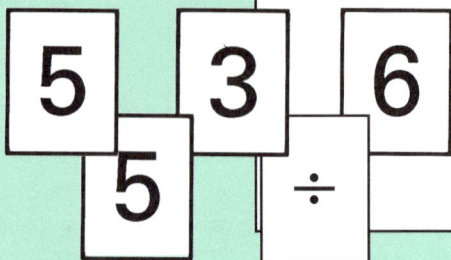

Learning the skill

Materials: Interlocking cubes.
Activity: Consider dividing a two-digit number by a one-digit number, for example, 48 ÷ 3. The children should understand that 48 ÷ 3 is more than 30 ÷ 3 = 10 and less than 60 ÷ 3 = 20 therefore the answer is between 10 and 20. Begin by splitting 48 into multiples of the divisor (30 + 18) ÷ 3, then divide each number by 3 and add the results to give the answer i.e. 30 ÷ 3 = 10, 18 ÷ 3 = 6, 10 + 6 = 16. Extend to answers with a remainder e.g. 72 ÷ 5. Split 72 into multiples of 5 (50 + 22 ⌉ 5), then divide each number by 5 (50 ÷ 5 = 10, 22 ÷ 5 = 4 remainder 2), and add the results (10 + 4 = 14 remainder 2).

Developing the skill

Materials: Number cards 0–9.
Activity: Reveal three cards to create a three-digit number, for example 553, and reveal a further card to find the divisor, for example 6, to create a division, i.e. 553 ÷ 6. Approximate the answer by saying 553 ÷ 6 is about 540 ÷ 6 = 90. Record the estimate, then split the three-digit number into multiples of the divisor (540 + 13) ÷ 6 and divide each number by 6 calculating any remainder:
553 ÷ 6 = (540 + 13) ÷ 6 = 90 + 2 r1 = 92 r1.
Repeat for other numbers.

Assessing the skill

Complete Unit 21 assessment.
If the child gets:
– ten or fewer answers correct, s/he should go to
  Reinforcing the skill
– eleven or more answers correct, s/he should move on to
  Extending the skill.

The answers to Unit 21 assessment are on page 48.

Reinforcing the skill

Materials: Base 10 material (hundreds, tens and ones).
Activity: Illustrate a division (for example 237 ÷ 7) as repeated subtraction. Collect two hundreds, three tens and seven ones in base 10 material, then exchange the hundreds for tens and subtract 70 (7 x 10) from the material and record. Repeat and continue until an amount less than 70 remains. Subtract the closest multiple of 7 from the final number to give a remainder. Count how many multiples of 7 were subtracted (33 remainder 6).

Extending the skill

Skill: To develop a standard method of division.
Materials: Number cards 0–9.
Activity: Shuffle the cards and reveal three cards to create a three-digit number e.g. 197. Reveal a further card to find the divisor e.g. 6 to create a division, i.e. 197 ÷ 6. Approximate by saying 197 ÷ 6 is about 200 ÷ 5 = 40, then proceed to divide by 6 in a standard way by saying 30 x 6 = 180. Subtract 180 from 197 to give 17 and find how many sixes in 17 by multiplying 6 x 2 = 12. Subtract 12 from 17 to give a remainder of 5. Record the answer as 32 remainder 5 and compare the answer with the estimate to check it is within the right region.

Dividing

Name _____

Complete:

1. **51 ÷ 3 =** ☐

    = (30 + 21) ÷ 3

    = 10 + 7

    =

    _____

2. **56 ÷ 4 =** ☐

    =

    =

    =

    _____

3. **98 ÷ 7 =** ☐

    =

    =

    =

    _____

4. **79 ÷ 6 =** ☐ r

    =

    =

    =   r

    _____

5. **98 ÷ 8 =** ☐ r

    =

    =

    =   r

    _____

6. **67 ÷ 5 =** ☐ r

    =

    =

    =   r

    _____

7. **225 ÷ 3 =** ☐

    = (210 + 15) ÷ 3

    = 70 + 5

    =

    _____

8. **460 ÷ 5 =** ☐

    =

    =

    =

    _____

9. **364 ÷ 7 =** ☐

    =

    =

    =

    _____

10. **259 ÷ 3 =** ☐ r

    =

    =

    =   r

    _____

11. **389 ÷ 6 =** ☐ r

    =

    =

    =   r

    _____

12. **569 ÷ 8 =** ☐ r

    =

    =

    =   r

    _____

13. **473 ÷ 9 =** ☐ r

    =

    =

    =   r

    _____

14. **513 ÷ 7 =** ☐ r

    =

    =

    =   r

    _____

15. **353 ÷ 4 =** ☐ r

    =

    =

    =   r

    _____

Answers

Unit 1

(1) Thirty thousand, six hundred and twenty-four (2) Twenty-six thousand, five hundred and thirty-two (3) Two hundred and fifty-two thousand and forty-seven (4) Five hundred and ninety-four thousand, five hundred and one (5) One million three hundred and seventy-seven thousand (6) 23 758 (7) 86 935 (8) 310 447 (9) 114 460 (10) 3 238 000 (11) 87 206 (12) 60 000 (13) 8000 (14) 400 (15) 40 (16) 1000 (17) 3 (18) 60 000 (19) 2000 (20) 400 000 (21) 50 000 (22) 10 (23) 500 000 (24) 5

Unit 2

(1) 1 000 000 (2) 3000 (3) 6 000 000 (4) 70 000 (5) 400 000 (6) 600 (7) 200 (8) 80 000 (9) 9000 (10) 500 000 (11) 600 (12) 500 (13) 70 000 (14) 7 (15) 10 (16) 20 (17) 4000 (18) 8000 (19) 90 000 (20) 30 (21) 10 (22) 10 (23) 100 (24) 10 (25) 60 000 (26) 4000 (27) 2000 (28) 100 (29) 10 (30) 10

Unit 3

(1) -3 (2) 1 (3) 5 (4) -7 (5) 8 (6) -5 (7) -5, -4, -2, -1, 1 (8) -10, -9, -7, -6, -5, (9) -4^0C (10) 1^0C (11) -1^0C (12) -8^0C (13) D

Unit 4

(1) 17 651 (2) 72 819 (3) 36 122 (4) 21 053 (5) 28 615 (6) 28 392 (7) > (8) < (9) < (10) > (11) <, > (12) >, < (13) to (23) Answers will vary.

Unit 5

Answers are approximate.
(1) 2000 (2) 4500 (3) 9250 (4) 5000 (5) 1500 (6) 6750 (7) 2000 (8) 4500 (9) 6250 (10) 1000 (11) 2500 (12) 4000 (13) -45 (14) -30 (15) -5

Unit 6

(1) 1590, 2000, 1600 (2) 1340, 1000, 1300 (3) 1870, 2000, 1900 (4) 1390, 1000, 1400 (5) 1080, 1000, 1100 (6) 1760, 2000, 1800 (7) 1940, 2000, 1900 (8) 1690, 2000, 1700 (9) 1440, 1000, 1400 (10) 1110, 1000, 1100 (11) 5000 (12) 6000 (13) 6000 (14) 7000 (15) 3500 (16) 1100 (17) 2600 (18) 4600

Unit 7

(1) even (2) odd (3) even (4) even (5) odd (6) odd (7) odd (8) odd (9) even (10) even (11) odd (12) even (13) odd (14) even (15) even (16) even (17) odd

Unit 8

(1) 16 (2) 49 (3) 81 (4) yes (5) yes (6) no (7) no (8) yes (9) no (10) yes (11) no (12) yes (13) 4 (14) 36 (15) 16 (16) 64 (17) 9 (18) 100 (19) 25 (20) 81 (21) 49 (22) 5 (23) 2 (24) 9 (25) 10 (26) 8 (27) 6 (28) 7 (29) 1 (30) 4

Unit 9

(1) 2, 3, 4, 6 (2) 2, 4, 7, 14 (3) 2, 3, 4, 6, 9, 12, 18 (4) 2, 4, 7, 8, 14, 28 (5) 2, 3, 4, 6, 8, 9, 12, 18, 24, 36 (6) 4 (7) 4 (8) 10 (9) 7 (10) 2 (11) 10 (12) yes (13) yes (14) yes (15) no (16) no (17) no (18) no (19) yes (20) yes (21) 1, 2, 3, 7, 11, 13, 17, 19, 21, 23, 29, 31, 37, 39, 41, 43, 47

Unit 10

(1) 17 (2) 24 (3) 12 (4) 4 (5) 9 (6) 9 (7) 12 (8) 26 (9) 12 (10) 8 (11) 9 (12) 50 (13) 24 (14) 10 (15) 24 (16) 8 (17) 27 (18) 25 (19) 18 (20) 8 (21) 21 (22) 70 (23) 60 (24) 9 (25) 240 (26) 40 (27) 24 (28) 56

Unit 11

(1) $\frac{45}{100}$, 0.45 (2) $\frac{83}{100}$, 0.83 (3) $1\frac{22}{100}$, 1.22 (4) 1.13 (5) 2.17 (6) 5.28 (7) 17.56 (8) 9.05 (9) 8.3 (10) $6\frac{32}{100}$ (11) $5\frac{75}{100}$ (12) $9\frac{84}{100}$ (13) $16\frac{41}{100}$ (14) $7\frac{3}{100}$ (15) $5\frac{20}{100}$ (16) 1.42, $1\frac{42}{100}$ (17) 1.65, $1\frac{65}{100}$ (18) 1.17, $1\frac{17}{100}$ (19) 1.91, $1\frac{91}{100}$ (20) 1.26, $1\frac{26}{100}$ (21) 1.54, $1\frac{54}{100}$

Unit 12

(1) 35.74 (2) 19.36 (3) 0.08 (4) 7 (5) 6 (6) 0.3 (7) 8 (8) 0.06 (9) 5 (10) 0.7 (11) 0.07 (12) 0.08 (13) 7 (14) 0.4 (15) 0.2 (16) 0.05 (17) 0.04 (18) 0.3 (19) 9 (20) 100 (21) 30 (22) 0.7 (23) 400 (24) 0.02 (25) 5 (26) 0.7

Unit 13

(1) 0.2, 1 (2) 0.4, 1 (3) 0.6, 2 (4) 0.9, 2 (5) 25.8, 26 (6) 22.9, 23 (7) 27.2, 27 (8) 21.2, 21 (9) 24.4, 24 (10) 28.6, 29 (11) 2 (12) 2 (13) 5 (14) 26 (15) 34 (16) 37 (17) 12 (18) 14 (19) 15 (20) 11

Unit 14

(1) $\frac{20}{100}$, 0.20 (2) $\frac{90}{100}$, 0.90 (3) $\frac{50}{100}$, 0.50 (4) 0.80, $\frac{80}{100}$ (5) 0.60, $\frac{60}{100}$ (6) 0.40, $\frac{40}{100}$ (7) 0.75 (8) 0.3 (9) 0.40 (10) $\frac{6}{10}$ (11) $\frac{9}{10}$ (12) $\frac{7}{10}$ (13) 0.20 (14) 0.42 (15) 0.6 (16) 0.1 (17) 0.70 (18) 0.93

Unit 15

(1) 40% (2) 90% (3) 25% (4) 50% (5) 75% (6) 70% (7) 60% (8) 10% (9) 20% (10) 30% (11) 25% (12) 80% (13) 1% (14) 60% (15) 50%

Unit 16

(1) £10 (2) £5 (3) £2 (4) £15 (5) £8 (6) £18 (7) £5 (8) £25 (9) £10 (10) £40 (11) £1 (12) £12.50 (13) £3 (14) £35 (15) £8 (16) £20 (17) £7.50 (18) £18 (19) £16 (20) £40 (21) £180 (22) £240

Unit 17

(1) 500, 560 (2) 800, 793 (3) 900, 982 (4) 900, 963 (5) 600, 625 (6) 700, 643 (7) 1000, 1020 (8) 700, 671 (9) 7000, 7410 (10) 3000, 3461 (11) 4000, 4155 (12) 7000, 6824 (13) 3 (14) 4 (15) 4 (16) 7 (17) 4, 6 (18) 4, 3 (19) 6, 5, 1 (20) 5, 5

Unit 18

(1) 100, 113 (2) 300, 312 (3) 700, 723 (4) 200, 156 (5) 200, 136 (6) 300, 314 (7) 200, 145 (8) 700, 639 (9) 300, 285 (10) 100, 74 (11) 300, 345 (12) 600, 579 (13) 2000, 2239 (14) 5000, 4399 (15) 3000, 2508 (16) 1000, 1338 (17) 4000, 3885 (18) 6000, 5689 (19) 2000, 1876 (20) 1000, 1488

Unit 19

(1) 5, 6, 30 (2) 7, 8, 56 (3) 14, 56, 28, 42, 6, 24, 12, 18, 10, 40, 20, 30, 2, 8, 4, 6 (4) 48, 64, 56, 72, 36, 48, 42, 54, 54, 72, 63, 81, 42, 56, 49, 63 (5) 24 (6) 40 (7) 28 (8) 36 (9) 21 (10) 70 (11) 30 (12) 42 (13) 9 (14) 6 (15) 4 (16) 3 (17) 7 (18) 7 (19) 9 (20) 3

Unit 20

(1) 90 (2) 23 x 6 = 138 (3) 42 x 7 = 294 (4) 36 x 5 = 180 (5) 2568 (6) 286 x 4 = 1144 (7) 423 x 5 = 2115 (8) 156 x 7 = 1092

Unit 21

(1) 17 (2) 14 (3) 14 (4) 13 r 1 (5) 12 r 2 (6) 13 r 2 (7) 75 (8) 92 (9) 52 (10) 86 r 1 (11) 64 r 5 (12) 71 r 1 (13) 52 r 5 (14) 73 r 2 (15) 88 r 1